The Essential Spirituality Handbook

WENDY M. WRIGHT, PhD

Liguori
LIGUORI, MISSOURI

Imprimi Potest:
Thomas D. Picton, C.Ss.R.
Provincial, Denver Province
The Redemptorists

Library of Congress Cataloging-in-Publication Data

Wright, Wendy M.
   The essential spirituality handbook / Wendy M. Wright. — 1st ed.
     p. cm.
   ISBN 978-0-7648-1786-1
   1. Spirituality—Catholic Church. 2. Catholic Church—Doctrines.
I.
Title.
   BX2350.65.W75 2009
   248.4'82--dc22

                           2009008834

Liguori Publications, a nonprofit corporation, is an apostolate of the Redemptorists. To learn more about the Redemptorists, visit Redemptorists.com.

To order, call 800-325-9521
www.liguori.org

Printed in the United States of America
13 12 11 10 09 5 4 3 2 1
First edition

Contents

Contents

Contents

Spirituality in the Catholic Tradition

You formed my inmost being:
You knit me in my mother's womb.
I praise you so wonderfully you have made me;
Wonderful are your works!
My very self you knew;
My bones were not hidden from you,
When I was being made in secret
fashioned as in the depths of the earth.
Your eyes foresaw my actions;
In your book all are written down;
My days were shaped, before one came to be.

PSALM 139:13–16

1. The Use of the Term "Spirituality" in the Contemporary World

The word "spirituality" is omnipresent in American society today. One cannot go into a bookstore or read a magazine article or attend a wellness program or a health seminar without some reference to spirituality. But to what does this actually refer? In fact, if you were to look for the term in a Catholic encyclopedia published before the late twentieth century, you wouldn't find an entry at all. You might find a listing under theology for a subset of that formal discipline, entitled "Spiritual and Moral Theology." You might also find reference to what is known as the "spiritual life." But what is implied in those terms is not necessarily what most people think about when they use the terms today.

If we turn to Scripture and the writings of Saint Paul, we discover that for him there were people, objects, actions, and thoughts which, if they were influenced by the Holy Spirit, could be considered spiritual. Paul also thought that all members of the Church, the body of Christ, shared in the holiness of Christ through baptism. Clearly, such people were "spiritual." They were intimately connected to the Divine through all the persons of the Trinity, the third person being the Holy Spirit.

The term "spiritual" was sometimes later used in different ways, as in the medieval era, when it referred to property that belonged to the Church rather than to other owners. It began to be used in a way that we might recognize in the seventeenth century, but it had a pejorative rather than a positive meaning. The French word *spiritualité* was coined to refer to the somewhat suspect interior prayer practices of certain groups, Quietists to be exact, who were out of favor at the time. Over the years, it has lost its pejorative connotation and emerged in our time as an oft-used term. Since the Second Vatican Council, in Catholic circles the term "spirituality" has generally replaced the older terms "ascetical" or "mystical theology." Unfortunately, in general popular usage, it also seems to have multiple and often vague meanings.

That the term has come a long way is apparent in the commonly heard phrase all over America today: "I'm spiritual but not religious." What this usually means is that a person wishing to define him or herself in this way is not affiliated with a religious community or has not discovered the religious community to be a place where the deeper longings of the heart are honored. They may feel that the faith traditions they have explored seem to be all about doctrine and ritual and not about soul care, or that religious people seem to be about making all sorts of judgments about who has it right and who doesn't. Underlying this typically American phenomenon, we recognize further definitional issues which are important to keep in mind.

2. A Theological Understanding of the Term

When people stand within the Christian tradition and talk about spirituality, usually they are making some very real theological assumptions. They assume that spirituality has something to do with the Holy Spirit, the third person of the Trinity, whom Christians believe was sent to the Church at

Pentecost to continue Christ's work in the world. The Holy Spirit is the giver of gifts meant to build up the community. The Catholic sacrament of confirmation is about an outpouring of spiritual gifts that deepen and confirm baptismal promises. Doctrines about the Holy Spirit and traditions that interpret just what these gifts are vary, but put simply, the Spirit works through human beings to inspire, guide, comfort, and enlighten. We acknowledge this in the liturgy of the feast of Pentecost when we sing or recite the great Pentecost Sequence. The feast celebrates the moment when, after the crucifixion, Jesus' traumatized disciples gathered together in the Upper Room (Acts 2:1–42), and the Spirit, in the form of mighty wind and tongues of fire, descended upon them and filled them with its power. This event, remembered as the beginning of the Church, points to the centrality of the Spirit in the life of Christian discipleship. This is the life to which all of us, not merely those gathered in the Upper Room twenty centuries ago, are heir. We are the ones Saint Peter spoke of at that time: "Repent and be baptized, every one of you, in the name of Jesus Christ for the forgiveness of your sins; and you will receive the gift of the Holy Spirit" (Acts 2:38). We are called to live in the Spirit. One of the great arts developed over the Christian centuries is the art of discerning the continuing movement of the Spirit, both in the individual and in the community, and distinguishing it from other sorts of impulses, movements, and ideas so that one can live authentically and in response to God's desire for one's life and the life of the world.

What this means is when most Christians use the term

"spirituality," they are implying that the Holy Spirit is dynamically involved in their lives.

3. Spirituality as Constitutive of the Human Condition

There are other ways that the term "spirituality" is used today; however, some of them are compatible with theological understandings, and some of them have very little to do with Christian theology. An example of the latter would be the notion that spirituality is synonymous with the style or "spirit" with which an individual or group goes about its particular way of being in the world. Thus each man or woman might be perceived as having a unique spirituality. There could be said to be a Midwestern spirituality, or a spirituality specific to ballet dancers, or an adolescent spirituality. This is a very general and vague notion.

It is also common to hear the term applied to mainly personal practices or holistic cosmo-visions of established religious communities. Hence, we could speak of a Buddhist, a Native American, a Jewish, and a Mormon spirituality. There are, however, ways to think about the term that are more anthropological (in the sense that they refer primarily to the human person) than theological. This does not preclude them from being useful ways to think about spirituality if you are a Catholic Christian. In fact, they can be very illuminating.

One contemporary person who uses the term this way and whose writings are familiar to many American Catholics through his daily columns that run in numerous diocesan newspapers is Father Ronald Rolheiser, OMI. In his popular book, *The Holy Longing*, Rolheiser suggests that every person has an inner fire, a desire, a holy longing:

> ...an unquenchable fire, a restlessness, a longing, a disquiet, a hunger, a loneliness, a gnawing nostalgia, a wildness that cannot be tamed, a congenital all-embracing ache that lies at the center of human experience and that is the ultimate force that drives everything else. This disease is universal. Desire gives no exceptions. ...Spirituality is, ultimately, what we do with that desire.
>
> THE HOLY LONGING:
> SEARCHING FOR A CHRISTIAN SPIRITUALITY

Note that for Rolheiser, spirituality is what we do with our inbuilt longing, which he would assume is fashioned in us as creatures made in the divine image and likeness (a foundational Christian idea). Others have defined spirituality in somewhat different but not incompatible ways. For example, Church historian Philip Sheldrake gives a broad definition, asserting that "the word 'spirituality' refers to the deepest values and meanings by which people seek to live. In other words, 'spirituality' implies some kind of vision of the human spirit and of what will assist it to achieve full potential" (*A Brief History of Spirituality*). Note that Sheldrake is not referencing the third person of the Trinity, but a dimension of the human person. (Sheldrake would also affirm the Holy Spirit, but here his definition focuses on the human experience and capacity to seek meaning and transcendence.)

Someone like Scripture scholar Sandra Schneiders glosses this notion by saying that there is no "generic" spirituality, only specific spiritual traditions, for example, Catholic or Methodist or Buddhist or liberationist. In other words, she is noting that spirituality is not a substance in and of itself, but is always linked to a set of ideas, practices, and insights like those generally found in established religious traditions or philosophies; it has content. But, like Rolheiser, both of these interpreters want to say there is something about human beings, some capacity for self-transcendence, some vaulting urge beyond simple existence that is compelling and deeply human. In another context, Schneiders talks about spirituality as an intentional process that involves the self-transcending integration of all an individual's capacities toward that which he or she perceives as ultimate. To study Christian spirituality then, which is what Schneiders does, involves the study of lived experience "as it actually transforms its subject toward fullness of life in Christ, that is, toward self-transcending life-integration within the Christian community of faith" ("The Study of Christian Spirituality: Contours and Dynamics of a Discipline").

If all this seems a bit academic, it might help to give some attention to what this book is about: Catholic spirituality. And because it is about something we have named spirituality, it is good to know from the beginning how the term is being used. For our purposes, in this particular moment in the history of the American Catholic Church, the term "spirituality" will be understood to be applicable in both the theological and anthropological senses. It will assume the dynamic action of God's Holy Spirit in the community of faith. It will also allude to the fact that human beings possess a restless spirit that urges them forward to fullness and potentiality. When historical figures are alluded to in the text, the reader can assume that past Catholic saints and sinners assumed the dynamic action of the Holy Spirit in the world. We postmodern American Catholics can assume that as well. But we can also use the term to refer to the inbuilt human capacity for self-transcendence and recognize in ourselves the restless holy longing for something more.

Some of our contemporaries may use the term anthropologically without reference to theology or to the Divine at all. But we can use it both ways. Our forebearers in the tradition might not have used the term "spirituality," but they did sense that there is a correspondence between the human spirit and the Holy Spirit. They would say that the human spirit is created by and for God, and that the divine Spirit inclines to us. We are "knit," as medieval English mystic Julian of Norwich would have it, to God in our creation:

> Before he made us he loved us. And when we were made, we loved him. And this is the love made of the natural, substantial goodness of the Holy Spirit; powerful by reason of the power of the Father, and wise in the wisdom of the Son. And thus man's soul is made by God, and at the same time knit to God.
>
> FROM *SHOWINGS*
> QUOTED IN *CHRIST OUR MOTHER: JULIAN OF NORWICH*

We believe in the intimacy of this union, for just as we are "knit" to God, so God is "knit" to us in taking flesh in Jesus the Christ.

Sources Cited

Pelphrey, Brant. *Christ Our Mother: Julian of Norwich*. Wilmington, DE: Michael Glazier, 1989.

Rolheiser, Ronald. *The Holy Longing: The Search for a Christian Spirituality*. New York: Doubleday, 1999.

Schneiders, Sandra M. "The Study of Christian Spirituality: Contours and Dynamics of a Discipline," *Minding the Spirit: The Study of Christian Spirituality*. Eds. Elizabeth A. Dreyer and Mark S. Burrows. Baltimore, MD: The Johns Hopkins University Press, 2005.

Sheldrake, Philip. *A Brief History of Spirituality*. Oxford/Malden, MA: Blackwell Publishing, 2007.

Further Reading: Classic and Contemporary

The Catechism of the Catholic Church, http://www.usccb.org/catechism/text/.

New American Bible with Revised New Testament and Revised Psalms © 1991, 1986, 1970 Confraternity of Christian Doctrine, Washington, D.C.

Note: There are many translations of the classic texts in the Catholic spiritual tradition suggested below and throughout this handbook. Some noteworthy series of translations that can be recommended are the Paulist Press Classics of Western Spirituality series, which has many of the texts cited published under the author's name; the Institute of Carmelite Studies series on Carmelite authors; the Cistercian Publications translations of Cistercian Fathers; and the Modern Spiritual Masters series, published in the United States by Orbis Books.

Julian of Norwich, *Showings*
Francis de Sales, *Treatise on the Love of God*

The Christic Pattern of the Catholic Spiritual Life

*For those who are led by the Spirit of God are children
of God. For you did not receive a spirit of slavery to
fall back into fear, but you received a spirit of adop-
tion through which we cry, Abba, "Father!"*

*The Spirit itself bears witness with our spirit that
we are children of God, and if children, then heirs,
heirs of God and joint heirs of Christ, if only we suffer with him so that we may also be glorified with
him.*

ROMANS 8:14–17

If spirituality is about the inbuilt capacity for life integration and self-transcendence toward that which is ultimate, then it might be helpful to consider the process by which such integration and self-transcendence takes place. We might come at this from a variety of perspectives, say, using the lens of any number of schools of psychology or other humanistic or social science disciplines. But, while these theoretical lenses might illuminate the process to some degree, they do not address the theological foundations that are assumed within the Catholic Christian tradition. Nor do they take into account the long history of wise reflection within Christianity upon this very topic. Indeed, if we affirm that God's Spirit acts within the world to transform it, then we can look to the theological tradition to discern what has been said about that process. The other disciplines—psychology, history, literature, the arts, and sociology among them—may then help illuminate this basic process. But the explication of how that might take place is another subject far beyond the scope of the present work. We will content ourselves here with the theological foundations for Catholic spirituality.

1. Human Beings Created in the Divine Image and Likeness, But Wounded

The starting point for any authentic Catholic spirituality is the knowledge that human beings are created by God, who is Love, in the divine image and likeness. We are made both by and for God. The rhapsodic words of the Song of Songs sing of this truth, this passionate love of God for humankind, and invite each of us to respond in kind.

Set me as a seal on your heart,
as a seal on your arm;
For stern as death is love,
relentless as the nether world is devotion;
its flames are a blazing fire.
Deep waters cannot quench love,
nor floods sweep it away.

SONG OF SONGS 8:6B–7A

We are loved with an inexpressible love, and we are designed to love God in return and to love others as we ourselves are loved.

The third chapter of the Gospel according to John makes the first affirmation clear: "For God so loved the world that he gave his only Son" (John 3:16a). The familiar "Two Commandments," spoken by Jesus to a scholar of the religious law who was questioning him, underscores the last part of this affirmation. "He said to him, 'You shall love the Lord your God, with all your heart, with all your soul, and with all your mind. This is the greatest and the first commandment. The second is like it: You shall love your neighbor as yourself'" (Matthew 22:37–39). We can see evidence of this truth for ourselves in our awareness of that unquenchable desire we all have and of which Fr. Rolheiser and others speak.

We can also see glimpses of this truth in human actions and creativity, both extraordinary and ordinary: in heroic sacrifice, in self-forgetful service and care, in art that ennobles, forgiveness that frees, and compassion that heals. But that divine image within us is not untarnished. It is wounded. The classic way to speak of this is to make reference to sin. We need only read the daily news to be saddened and disturbed by the depths to which human beings can sink. And a search of our own hearts must reveal that each of us, in great or small ways, fails to live in the fullness of life for which we were created. While this is so, our Catholic faith nevertheless affirms that the love which created, sustains, and compels us is stronger than sin and death itself.

God's inexhaustible love extends into the depths of the wounded human condition in the person of Jesus the Christ. Hence, we are offered salvation through Jesus' incarnation, passion, death, and ultimate resurrection. This is the core of our Catholic faith. But the importance of the Christ event does not end there. The tarnished divine image and likeness in each of us can be progressively cleansed, our wounds gradually healed, not only through the graces available through the sacraments, but through our responsiveness to the creative, restorative prompting of the Holy Spirit. The Spirit is alive and moving among us to facilitate all sorts of personal and communal transformation. We can be sanctified and grow in holiness and grace. It might help explain these traditional ideas to say: We are at root spiritual people who, despite the fact that we do not always live into that truth, still long for more. By listening to the deepest longings of our hearts, learning from the wisdom of tradition and engaging in spiritual practices, and held by the ground of love at the core of all that is, we can grow into spiritually mature persons. We, as human beings, are fundamentally about spirituality.

2. Jesus the Paradigm: Death and Resurrection

The process of this spiritual maturation, while not entirely of our own doing, is not random. It is patterned on the arc of Christ's actions, revealed to us in the Gospel narratives. In other words, as unique and unrepeatable in detail as it might be in any individual case, there is a classic pattern to the Catholic spiritual life. Jesus' life, death, and resurrection provide the pattern.

The shape of that pattern is kenotic, a Greek word that means emptiness. Scripture tells us that Jesus' life was kenotic. Saint Paul in his letter to the church at Philippi puts it this way:

> *Have among yourselves the same attitude*
> *that is also yours in Christ Jesus, Who,*
> *though he was in the form of God,*
> *did not regard equality with God*
> *something to be grasped.*
> *Rather, he emptied himself,*
> *taking the form of a slave,*
> *coming in human likeness;*
> *and found human in appearance,*
> *he humbled himself,*
> *becoming obedient to death,*
> *even death on a cross.*

PHILIPPIANS 2:5–8

Paul, of course, is making some very significant theological claims about who Jesus is. But the basic intuition is that as Christians, followers of Christ, we do not simply have beliefs about Christ; we participate in a radical way in the Christ event. We take on not only the results of the mysteries played out in the life, death, and resurrection of Jesus of Nazareth; we take on, as it were, the very energy and dynamic of those events and continue to live into them, both for ourselves and for the world.

The self-emptying that we are called to embrace has as many forms as there are people. Thus it will never look the same, but be played out in innumerable ways in different eras, cultures, and geographical settings. A fourth-century hermit fasting in the deserts of Egypt, a twelfth-century German abbess composing liturgical songs, a seventeenth-century French housewife practicing devotion, a nineteenth-century Vietnamese priest beheaded for his faith, and a twentieth-century journalist serving soup to the hungry in the bowery district of New York would not seem, at first glance, to have much in common. But each one was, in his or her own way, living into the mystery of the kenotic process, the dying and rising with Christ that was asked of them in their discrete circumstances.

The process of self-emptying should not be mistaken for a sort of gloomy, psychologically questionable hatred of self or the created world. It is best not seen as deserved punishment or involving unbearable misery. Nor should it turn into a self-righteous opportunity to feel superior to others who seem less serious about their Christian commitment. Rather, it should be recalled that the process of kenosis is one that begins and ends in Love. God's own self-emptying to incline to the created order in Jesus was prompted by love, just as Jesus' death was an act of inexpressible love. So it is with the process as we experience it.

There are many ways of describing the emptying process. It may be viewed as sacrifice, as self-donation, as making space for God, as dying to the false self, as surrendering to divine providence, as discipline, or as moving from self-centeredness to other-centeredness. All these and other descriptions hit the mark. A familiar and apt analogy might be the self-emptying that caring parents undergo when their lives are de-centered by the needs of their children. Such de-centering is done, one hopes, in and for love of the other. This last example does not imply that the emerging spaciousness created by the process of self-emptying is easily won or trite. Far from it. It involves real suffering. Any process of shedding or dying, whether it be physical, psychological, or spiritual, can be challenging, arduous, and life-altering.

Ultimately, of course, the process is a transformative one. Jesus' death on the cross was not an end, but the beginning of radical newness, new life, new hope, a new world. So too our deaths, the kenotic pattern of our self-emptyings, with whatever specifics that accompany them (and these are legion), are preludes to the fullness of life that God promises for us. They make us the people God intended us to be. They usher us into Easter joy.

3. Classic Ways of Imaging the Spiritual Life

We have suggested that while the basic pattern of the Catholic Christian spiritual life is kenotic, there are innumerable variations on that theme. Another way to say this is to suggest that over the centuries, any number of metaphors have shaped the way that Christians imagine and hence experience the transforming movement of the Spirit in their lives.

PURGATION, ILLUMINATION, AND UNION

One of the most ancient metaphors, one that goes back to the era of the church fathers, is the description of the spiritual life as proceeding in three stages of Purgation, Illumination, and Union. These stages are not necessarily linear, but may occur over and over again as one's spirituality matures. Purgation involves peeling away, suffering, dying, making space. It is the preparation for illumination, for glimpses into who God is and what God intends for us. Illumination in turn prepares us for an ever deepening intimate union with the divine.

Perhaps a homey, even ordinary, analogy, along with another more spiritually focused consideration, might illustrate the dynamic of purgation. If one dreams of some day becoming a doctor, one must be prepared to make sacrifices. Medical school is a long, difficult academic track which requires a student who hopes to attend to align his or her priorities and give up some of the casual distractions of undergraduate life. Endless hours are spent in the library and in labs. If one is admitted to medical school, the hours spent in study and interning are long. The process may be painful, exhausting, and discouraging, but necessary in order to adequately prepare for the career ahead, one in which human lives often hang in the balance. The point here is that sacrifice, self-discipline and effort are part of any preparation. The future physician is not only acquiring knowledge and skills, but is also giving up a great deal else. The process of purgation may be something like this.

Another, more spiritually focused, analogy might come from a painful self-revelatory experience. Perhaps a woman considers herself to be very helpful and frequently goes out of her way to aid neighbors or friends. Perhaps in one case, a friend who objectively does not really need help may rebuff this helpful woman, and she finds herself very offended. She first tries to insist that the friend accept help; then she becomes angry and blames the friend for ingratitude. She cuts off contact and broods. Perhaps the motives of the helpful woman could be examined this way: Is she helping others because they need help? Because she selflessly serves? Because she habitually tries to earn others' love? Because she likes to think of herself as righteous or better than others who, she is quick to point out, are unhelpful? Though she may resist the insight into her motives, perhaps the woman begins to observe herself, to reach down into the ego-driven actions that have shaped her identity. Perhaps, painfully, she discovers that she is quite judgmental, or that she is unsure of herself and feels as if she has to always win the love of others by being (overly and intrusively) helpful. The point here is not that being helpful is necessarily a negative—quite the contrary, it might be a valid goal for any Christian—but that this woman had begun the process of purgation on the psychological and spiritual plane. What might follow would be illuminative glimpses—perhaps of the generosity of others whom she had previously written off. Perhaps she might be moved to pray and discover the God who loves her not for what she does, but simply because she is.

Purgation and the resulting illumination can take many forms: spiritual, physical, psychological, relational, and social. Sometimes purgation is chosen—the discipline of the medical school student or the serious spiritual practitioner come to mind—sometimes it is thrust upon us. Sometimes it is catalyzed by a traumatic loss or diminishment. Whatever way it comes, it involves growth and potentially creates spaciousness and a more generous heart. Illumination, as suggested, involves the glimpses of light and insight that illuminate our journeys. Union is the marriage of our capacities, to use the classic formulation, of our memory, understanding, and will with God. This is something we seek and long for all our lives. It is never achieved without some stripping process, some demanding process of change and growth. It would finally involve, to use the language of the heart, our leaning continually against the breast of Jesus like John the beloved disciple at the Last Supper, in such an intimate way that we could hear and feel the beat of his Sacred Heart so that our heart would beat with his.

ASCENT

Another ancient metaphor which is time honored is the image of "ascent." The spiritual life is often conceived as rising above the plain on which one at present stands. One of the classic treatises on spirituality comes from the sixth century and the pen of Saint John Climacus, a holy man living on Mount Athos in Greece. His Ladder of Divine Ascent describes the steps involved in raising one's soul and body to God as if on a ladder, the goal of which is *theosis* or mystical union with God. John clearly conceives of the process of transformation using the image of ascent. Other famed writings utilize this same metaphor. Another John, the sixteenth-century Spanish Carmelite, authored the incomparable guide, *Ascent of Mount Carmel* (which properly speaking, also includes the saint's other classic, *Dark Night of the Soul*). He emphasizes the path of negation by which the Christian must journey, a path that is, in its early instances especially, conceived as an ascending one.

Sometimes the ascent or ladder image describes a simultaneous descent and ascent. Saint Benedict of Nursia, founder of Benedictine monasticism, wrote about humility using the image of such a ladder. Drawn from the image of Jacob, who had a dream of a ladder upon which angels descended and ascended (Genesis 28), Benedict's ladder has twelve steps of humility that include practices such as reverence, surrendering to God's will, patient endurance, radical self-honesty, and restraint of speech, which at the same time humble one and bring one closer to God. The ascent metaphor orients us to God as transcendent and to the spiritual work involved in climbing eagerly upward.

JOURNEY AND PILGRIMAGE

Another metaphor suggests a quite different but very pervasive way of envisioning spiritual progress—as a journey or pilgrimage. In this metaphor, God is horizon, that which is ahead, but not yet attained. In fact, the journey metaphor often is used to suggest that it is not a destination that is desirable, but the journey itself. Discovered along the way are the pebbles on the path, the strangers met, the adventures encountered; these are the stuff of the journey. This metaphor is in popular use today, but the idea of travel, of moving from one place to a hoped-for destination, has long captured the imagination of generations of spiritually minded folks. The great Saint Augustine, bishop of Hippo, wrote of two cities in his monumental City of God: the city of the world and the heavenly city, to both of which all human beings in a sense belong, according to the direction of their love and longing. True citizens of the heavenly city, the bishop asserted, as long as they are in the body and in time, are in fact pilgrims in a foreign land, walking by faith and not by sight. Life is an unfinished journey to someplace we long to inhabit, but whose landscape we have not yet fully explored.

The journey may be through the foreign territory of the present city, as it was for Augustine, or it may be an interior journey. Using the image of an early modern castle, Spanish mystic Teresa of Ávila wrote of prayer as a movement through an interior castle. She was shown, in a vision, a globe of crystal in the shape of a castle containing seven rooms arranged in a sort of concentric circle, at the center of which was the King of Glory bathed in light. Each room, for Teresa, represented a stage on the journey of deepening prayer; each room contained its own experiences and led the journeyer closer to the brilliant center where the King dwelt. Teresa's metaphors, not only of the castle but of the various rooms, have entered the vocabulary of Catholic contemplative and mystical literature. She speaks of the interior movement in prayer, using the metaphor of two fountains, when God, rather than the one praying, initiates the relationship. One fountain is filled with water from afar, conduits or aqueducts being used to transport it, a task which requires great human effort. The other fountain is constructed at the site of a well; the water source does not require human engineering to flow freely. Just so, Teresa teaches, is the Prayer of Quiet, a stage on the spiritual journey during which God, the source, rather than the one praying, initiates the activity. Similarly, deep into her castle, Teresa describes the Prayer of Union by using the metaphor of a silkworm which, feeding on mulberry leaves, spins and hides in an ugly cocoon, only to emerge later as a beautiful butterfly. It flies freely above the things that had previously kept it aground. The butterfly metaphor of effortless flight, of beauty, and of transformation is one of Teresa's gifts to the tradition.

SPIRITUAL WARFARE

Spiritual warfare, another ancient metaphor, frequently likens the process of spiritual transformation to a battle. The early desert dwellers of Syria, Egypt, and Palestine, whose sayings hold pride of place among early spiritual writings, described the purgative dimension of the Christian life in terms of a battle against "demons," the majority of whom were discovered in the human heart. Pride, lust, self-aggrandizement, greed, anger: these were the demons the ascetics sought to conquer through mortification and self-discipline. The battle was both interior and exterior, and victory was the death of the "old self" and the birth of the "new self" in Christ. Saint Anthony of Egypt, that quintessential ascetic, visited in his hermit's lair by personified demons of lust in the form of tempting females, is a favorite image in western Christian art. The warfare against the demons theme is still heard today, but it is good to recall that, in the desert literature, Anthony and his compatriots have the power of Christ with them, not simply their own wits. He is shown overcoming those powers that would assail him not out of fear and anger, but with the mysterious power of love that comes from the source of love itself. This reminds us that, in the words of the Song of Songs, "Deep waters cannot quench love, nor floods sweep it away" (8:7).

NUPTIAL AND MARRIAGE

Quite in keeping with this rapturous affirmation, nuptial or marriage imagery has also often been used to describe the spiritual process. From that most beautiful of biblical books, the Songs of Songs, lovers of God have long culled tender phrases and images to give voice to what they experience of the God of love. God is frequently addressed as the bridegroom, sought with longing by the bride. Examples are many: Saint Bernard of Clairvaux, in the twelfth century, taking his cue from the opening line of the Song, "Let him kiss me with the kisses of his mouth!" (Song of Songs 1:2), preached beautifully of the encounter with the Divine using the language of kisses. Kissing the groom's feet was an analogy for the purgative stage, the kiss on the hand spoke of illumination, and the kiss of the mouth of intimate union. Thirteenth century women mystics like Hadewijch of Brabant and Gertrude the Great of Helfta wrote of the ecstasy of encounter in mystic prayer and the agony of experiencing separation from the divine lover.

Today the language of loving intimacy easily becomes an analogy for divine love. American Trappist monk William Meninger tells the story of going to his abbot distraught that the loving search for God, which was the reason he had entered the monastery, was so difficult. He left the study of the wise abbot with a new perspective:

> ...[I]f you desire to love God, to meet and embrace God in the loving union of contemplative prayer, it means that God desires this union also. The invitation came from God; it was not your idea at all.... Is that not wonderful? Before you call upon God in prayer, God is already present to us, empowering us by the grace of the Holy Spirit to seek God. This is what I mean when I say that the loving search is, first of all, God's search for us....
>
> When you understand this, what difference does it make how much you have to struggle? You know it is worth it. You know who calls you, who accom-

panies you, and who is at the end of your loving
search.

THE LOVING SEARCH FOR GOD

Meninger would still face the difficulty of his quest to know
divine intimacy, but he had come to realize the value of the
struggle.

DARKNESS AND UNKNOWING

The entry into darkness where one loses sight or knowledge
can also serve as a metaphor for the spiritual process. The
anonymous English author of the Cloud of Unknowing situ-
ates his prayerful fourteenth century reader between a cloud
of forgetting that shields him from the world and a cloud of
unknowing that veils him from images and thoughts about
God. In this state of divine darkness, a single simple word, a
dart of love flung from the human heart, is all that pierces
the darkness.

In like manner, Dionysius the Areopagite, an early Syrian Christian whose writings profoundly influenced the later
Catholic spiritual imagination, wrote in his treatise, *Mystical
Theology*, of divine darkness. Using as his example Moses' ascent up Mount Sinai as recorded in the Scriptures, Dionysius
said that the one who prays deeply, after ascending through
the sensate and intelligible contemplation of God, enters the
darkness above the mountain's peak where union with God
in God's essence, inaccessible to human sight, speech, or
comprehension, is achieved. And of course, Carmelite master
Saint John of the Cross, during the early modern era, wrote

in his *Ascent of Mount Carmel* and *Dark Night of the Soul* of the love-driven ascent to the Divine, which is simultaneously an entry into darkness of both the senses and the spirit, a process of profound undoing and unknowing. The metaphor of darkness highlights the essentially unknowable mystery of God. Human cognition and language fail. Only the holy longing, the movement of love, can begin to approach God in God's essence.

These cited examples do not exhaust the metaphors used in the long Catholic tradition to give articulation to the process of spiritual transformation. We might well consider other hallowed metaphors such as contest, a race, childhood, poverty, surrender, or friendship. But the ones mentioned do suggest some of the richness and diversity to be discovered there.

We belong to a tradition of great depth and breadth that has given us a profusion of images with which to name the process of encounter with the Spirit. We are heirs to an infinitely expressive vocabulary created by Christians of many eras and locales.

Within myself I feel the inability to perform an act of perfect love, following Jesus on Calvary, dying with him on the Cross.

Thousands and thousands of years may pass and my position may not change. But…what is impossible for me, the rich man in the Gospel, is possible for God! It is he who will give me the grace to transform myself; he will make me able to carry out the impossible and remove the obstacle which separated me from the kingdom. And so it is a question of waiting, of humble and trustful prayer, of patience and hope. But the God of the impossible won't ignore my cry.

CARLO CARRETTO, *LETTERS FROM THE DESERT*
QUOTED IN *SELECTED WRITINGS*

Our own contemporary ways of speaking of the Spirit encounter, that kenotic process, are part of a larger reality, an ever-evolving and living organism, the Body of Christ. And in that Body, we are never alone.

Sources Cited

Carlo Carretto: Selected Writings. Ed. Robert Ellsberg. Modern Spiritual Masters Series. Maryknoll, NY: Orbis Books, 1994.

Meninger, William A., OCSO. *The Loving Search for God.* New York: Continuum, 1995.

New American Bible with Revised New Testament and Revised Psalms © 1991, 1986, 1970 Confraternity of Christian Doctrine, Washington, D.C.

Further Reading: Classic and Contemporary

The Blackwell Companion to Catholicism. Eds. Frederick Christian Bauerschmidt, James Buckley, and Trent Pomplun. Oxford/Malden, MA: Blackwell Publishers, 2007.

Muto, Susan. *Catholic Spirituality from A to Z: An Inspirational Dictionary.* Ann Arbor, MI: Charis Books, Servant Publications, 2000.

Note: There are many translations of the classic texts in the Catholic spiritual tradition suggested below and throughout this handbook. Some noteworthy series of translations that can be recommended are the Paulist Press Classics of Western Spirituality series, which has many of the texts cited published under the author's name; the Institute of Carmelite Studies series on Carmelite authors; the Cistercian Publications translations of Cistercian Fathers; and the Modern Spiritual Masters series, published in the United States by Orbis Books.

Anonymous, *The Cloud of Unknowing*

Athanasius, *Life of Antony of Egypt*

Augustine of Hippo, *City of God*

Benedict of Nursia, *The Rule of Saint Benedict*

Dionysius the Areopagite, *Mystical Theology*

Francis de Sales, *Treatise on the Love of God*

Gertrude of Helfta (the Great), *Herald of Divine Love*

Hadewijch of Brabant, *Poems*

John Climacus, *Ladder of Divine Ascent*

John of the Cross, *Ascent of Mount Carmel* and
   Dark Night of the Soul

Teresa of Ávila, *Interior Castle*

SECTION THREE

Belonging to the Mystical Body

As a body is one though it has many parts, and
all the parts of the body, though many, are one
body, so also Christ. For in one Spirit we were all
baptized into one body, whether Jews or Greeks,
slaves or free persons, and we were all given to
drink of one Spirit.

1 CORINTHIANS 12:12–13

1. The Vine and the Branches: The Church as Mystical Body

The fourteenth century was a turbulent one for European society and for the Church. There were plagues, famines, and wars that disrupted civil life and scandals that rocked the Church. In the midst of the chaos, a young Italian woman, Catherine of Siena, who was later named a saint and doctor of the Church—someone whose teachings capture the essence and fullness of the faith—spoke prophetically. She ached, she said, for the world and did not want anyone to forget the deepest truths of their lives: that they were children of an infinitely loving God and intimately connected to one another in a radical way. Each baptized person was truly a part of the Mystical Body of Christ.

The idea of the Body of Christ was not new in Catherine's day. Saint Paul, in his letters to the early followers of Jesus at Corinth, Ephesus, and Colossae, explains that the Church is more than an institution or a gathering of persons who share a vision. At baptism we became part of Christ's very life and, as such, continue his redeeming activity in the world. We are part of something larger than ourselves at a very deep level. Like a physical body, consisting of a head that guides the arms, legs, and so forth, the Church has Christ as its head and its members as the various parts.

For Catherine of Siena, like Saint Paul, the Mystical Body of Christ was not a pious figure of speech, but an astonishing reality. In her book, *The Dialogue,* she used the image of a vineyard to help her readers understand the nature of the

Mystical Body. Christ is the central, living vine onto which we are each engrafted when we are baptized. The Church is thus a vital, organic reality.

As part of this reality, each member has a vineyard, watered and nurtured by the graces that flow from the sacraments, especially the Eucharist. Although each of us has our own vineyard, no fences separate the vineyards, and whatever happens in our own little vineyard affects all the other vine growers, just as what each of them does affects us. Whatever fruits we receive—those gifts or graces given to us as we are nurtured in the vineyard—are not meant just for us. They are for the flourishing of all, and ultimately for the world. Being a part of a vast vineyard, this membership in the Body of Christ is our deepest identity. Yet this shared life never diminishes our individuality. All of us are created to be ourselves, to be the flowers in the garden that no one else can be. We each have our own history and our unique path to follow in the Body. Saint Francis de Sales, in the seventeenth century, said it this way: "Be what you are and be that well!"

2. Scripture and Tradition

Catherine of Siena sets the stage for our understanding of Catholic spirituality, for she emphasizes an essential aspect of it: that the common life, the shared life, our interconnection and interdependence with one another is foundational. Too often spirituality is perceived as something private and individualized. While it is emphatically true that spirituality is intensely personal and distinctive, Catholic spirituality is at the same time keenly attuned to the reality of God's world and God's people and the ways in which individuals are made for community and designed to care for and share with one another.

While as members of the Body of Christ, that vast vineyard, we each do our part and cultivate our own gardens as we are able, we also have a common story that we tell and a common ritual language that connects us to the deep truths of our lives. We Catholics, of course, have the Scriptures; they provide the stories and poetry with which to understand who we are and what it means to live well. From the majestic narratives of creation in Genesis to the awe-inspiring images of the Book of Revelation, the Bible paints word pictures for us that tell of God's infinite love, care, and mercy. The four Gospels especially offer us evidence of divine desire and intent in the narratives about Jesus the Christ. The Bible is central to Catholic spirituality; it is the bedrock upon which our faith rests. But we also trust that God's inspiring Spirit continues to act in history through the community of the Church. The wisdom of that cumulative historical activity is also held to have authority. Put simply, we honor both Scripture and tradition.

Tradition takes many forms, including dogmas, creeds, theological reflections, rituals, practices, or customs. Tradition is also understood to be living, not dead. Thus we participate in a vital, living community of faith. As the Catechism of the Catholic Church confirms: " 'In order that the full and living Gospel might always be preserved in the Church, the apostles left bishops as their successors. They gave them their own position of teaching authority.' Indeed, 'the apostolic preaching, which is expressed in a special way in the inspired books, was to be preserved in a continuous line of succession until the end of time.'

"This living transmission, accomplished in the Holy Spirit, is called Tradition, since it is distinct from Sacred Scripture, though closely connected to it. Through Tradition, 'the Church, in her doctrine, life, and worship perpetuates and transmits to every generation all that she herself is, all that she believes.' 'The sayings of the holy Fathers are a witness to the life-giving presence of this Tradition, showing how its riches are poured out in the practice and life of the Church, in her belief and her prayer'" (CCC 77–78).

We are the inheritors of a tradition that develops even as it stays firmly rooted in its deepest intuitions.

We can see how tradition works through consideration of the lives of the saints and founders of spiritual movements. Twentieth century Jesuit theologian Karl Rahner spoke of it this way: Christ is the inexhaustible, ever-evolving fountain of holiness from which the Church's holiness flows; in each era the saints are the pioneers who allow new streams of that life-giving fountain to burst forth. They embody that holiness in new and often daring ways.

The earlier streams continue to flow, but each new period of history calls for innovation, exploration, and creativity. It has been noted that all the founders of the great spiritual schools have their own favorite scriptural passage or image that has inspired them. They flesh out for us in each era what the Christ-life might look like in changing circumstances. They embody and incarnate the Christ-life in their present, varied circumstances. Thus, the hermits and monastics of the Egyptian, Syrian, and Palestinian deserts gave expression to the Christian life in the church's early years by imitating Jesus' days of temptation in the wilderness as described in each of the first three synoptic Gospels (Matthew 4, Mark 1, Luke 4). These ascetics gave up the pride, luxury, and self-aggrandizement of the social world from which they came in order, through spiritual and physical struggle, to become people of constant prayer, humility, purity of heart, and compassion.

SIXTH CENTURY

In fact, Saint Benedict called his monastery a "school for the service of the Lord." Monasteries still flourish and educate Christians for service and to live the Christ life, but changing circumstances have called forth different models of the Christ life.

THIRTEENTH CENTURY

In a similar manner, but reflecting on the Gospel in his own way, Saint Francis of Assisi, during the thirteenth century, literally performed the Gospel life in his radical poverty, inspired by the Gospel accounts of the poor, naked baby in the manger (Luke 2) and the naked, cross-hung crucified One (described in each of the Gospel accounts). Francis literally embodied this poor Christ. He refused to wear fine clothing, carry money, or seek any position or office of authority. Francis spoke of perfect joy and perfect identification with Christ in being unrecognized, cast out, and yet still welcoming of this experience. For him, it was poverty, God's nakedness as the Divine came among us, that was central—just as the struggle in the wilderness was central for the early ascetics.

SEVENTEENTH CENTURY

Focusing on a different Scripture, Saint Vincent de Paul found that the meaning of the Christ life was best captured in Luke's version of the inauguration of Jesus' ministry when he stood up in the synagogue and proclaimed Isaiah's words: "The Spirit of the Lord is upon me, because he has anointed me to bring good tidings to the poor. He has sent me to proclaim liberty to captives and recovery of sight to the blind, to let the oppressed go free, and to proclaim a year acceptable to the Lord" (Luke 4:18–19). For Vincent, the Christian life was shaped by that imperative as he rescued the abandoned infants and the destitute of seventeenth century Paris and worked for the release of galley slaves.

In the same century, the Savoyard bishop of Geneva, Saint Francis de Sales, was struck by the image of Jesus in Matthew 11: "Come to me...learn from me, for I am meek and humble of heart" (28–29). This became for him the center of his spiritual vision. De Sales taught that the task of the Christian was to "live Jesus" by practicing the little virtues such as gentleness and humility, so that one's heart would be transformed by and into the heart of Christ.

NINETEENTH CENTURY

A similar vision was put forward in nineteenth century Europe, with industrialization and urbanization pressing the population. Pioneers like Saints Don Bosco and Mary Mazzarello founded innovative, collaborative communities of priests, women religious, and lay persons to serve the Lord by ministering to impoverished boys living on the streets and by providing shelters for young working girls at risk. They too looked to the gentle humble Jesus of Matthew 11 and to the inspiration of Bishop de Sales as they developed a gentle, nurturing approach to dealing with street children.

TWENTIETH CENTURY

Finally, in twentieth-century Latin America, the Old Testament story of the Israelites' exodus from Egypt (Exodus 12) became, in part, the inspiration for the liberation spirituality of theologians like Gustavo Gutierrez. Liberation theology finds in Scripture a template for pastoral action on behalf of the poor and oppressed.

In the United States, in the same era, the Catholic Worker Movement arose, inspired by the scriptural vision of the judgment of the nations imaged in Matthew 25. There the Son of Man is pictured in glory, separating those who will inherit the kingdom at the last days from those who will be cast out. The litmus test for this separation is whether those being judged have welcomed the stranger, fed the hungry, clothed the naked, given drink to the thirsty, and visited those in prison. Thus the practice of these things, commonly known as the corporal works of mercy, became the basis for the spiritual vision of the Catholic Worker houses of hospitality where the homeless and poor are welcomed.

All this is part of the developing tradition of the Church,

the way in which both Scripture and the unfolding wisdom derived from living deeply into the Word of God are essential to Catholic spirituality. In the process, the unfolding mystery of the Spirit in the world is visible.

3. Common Prayer

Catholic Christian spirituality is rooted in Scripture and tradition. Part of that tradition involves shared or common prayer. When Jesus was asked by his disciples how to pray, they were not simply asking for instructions in a method of addressing God. They were asking, "How should we pray? How should we, who follow you and share with you the divine Father, speak?" He taught them a common prayer, the Lord's Prayer. The Pater Noster, as it is known in its Latin translation, is not only the most familiar of prayers, it is perhaps the most frequently recited. It has a privileged place in the Eucharistic liturgy and in the Liturgy of the Hours, as well as in paraliturgical services. And, over the centuries, this Our Father has been received and commented on as the most perfect of prayers, containing every element of the faith.

As early as the turn of the third century, the apologist for the Christian faith, Tertullian, wrote that this prayer contained all the instructions of Jesus and was, in fact, a summary of the Gospel. Commentaries have flourished over the decades, and the prayer continues to inspire contemporary spiritual writers. Jesuit Michael Kennedy, who has spent much of his ministry working among the poor in the barrios of East Los Angeles, imagines himself, in his meditation on the version of Jesus' prayer found in the Gospel of Luke, as

Peter watching Jesus pray, questioning him and receiving a response:

...jesus
i watched as you prayed
i ask you
to teach me
to pray like you do

peter
look at what
we saw
when we went
to the temple yesterday
the loud voices
repeating
psalm after psalm
the demanding of certain needs
so peter
you ask me
how you speak
with the one
whom you love
for me
I need to be
with my abba
in order
to keep the vision
of how

to do his will
we do not need
to say so many words
but
to be in our abba's presence
listening
to what he desires
for us
very simple

EYES ON JESUS: A GUIDE FOR CONTEMPLATION

Individual prayer, of course, can and should be intensely personal, even idiosyncratic. But when we pray together, we are doing so both as individuals and as a community. The practice of praying together both informs us and forms us. It allows us to grow into a shared sense of identity and purpose. It creates such community not only in space, across the globe, but in time, across the centuries. For when we pray the Lord's Prayer, we are praying in concert with our forefathers and mothers in faith and with all those who will follow us. Prayer is not just a present utterance. Prayer ushers us into divine time, into the presence of the eternal. There we find ourselves at one with all who are held in love in the heart of God.

COMMON EUCHARISTIC PRAYER

There are several patterns of shared prayer that bind us as a Catholic people. The first, of course, is the Eucharistic liturgy. No matter where you go on the globe, no matter in what local language it is offered, and no matter what style of music accompanies it, the pattern of the Catholic Mass is the same worldwide. This has been basically true, with some allowance for historical variation, for much of the long life of the Church. It is certainly true today. We share a table, we are nourished by the same body and blood, and we participate in the same, ever-fresh yet ancient ritual encounter. Our identities as citizens of nation-states, members of families, speakers of English, Chinese, Dutch, or Spanish, while very important, are secondary to our identities as children of God and members of the Body of Christ. In the eucharistic liturgy we affirm and act out our shared identity. The wonderful feast of Christ the King, which occurs at the close of the Church year, is a culminating celebration of our shared life under the protective divine mantle. It is a celebration both of the abundant reign of God to which we are heir, but also of the universality of the Church's life, which dwarfs our historical and cultural differences.

This sense of a common life deeply informs Catholic spirituality. We are not simply in it for ourselves, for our personal salvation or sanctification, we are in it for the common good. When, in parishes around the United States, the feast of Christ the King is celebrated in Tagalog or Vietnamese or Spanish or English, we celebrate a unity which transcends language and cultural inheritance, yet which does not obliterate our differences. The Eucharist affirms our common life in many ways. At the center of the Eucharist, we share a common meal. Christ becomes our food and drink, which nourishes all of us. And, as we are nourished, we become what we eat.

How different this is from the way in which we often experience ourselves in relation to other people! We generally have a circle of intimates, family and friends, with whom we might share a common meal, with whom we identify and experience oneness. Others are often left outside the circle. But the eucharistic liturgy invites us into a deeper sense of who we are. All of us, gathered around one table at which Christ is present, share a kinship. In fact, the Eucharist invites us even further: to know ourselves as part of a divine creation, connected to all other creatures and to God's good creation, and called to love as we have been loved. In the words of Psalm 98, sung often in the season of Easter, "All the ends of the earth have seen the power of God."

Although Catholics may participate in the Eucharist most any day of the week, the Sunday Eucharist is paramount on the liturgical calendar. Early Christians designated Sunday as the Lord's day. It was celebrated in honor of the resurrection, marked the beginning of each week, and was described as the eighth day. This was significant because it signaled to those early Christians that with the resurrection, a new sort of dispensation had begun. A new life was offered; a new vision of themselves and the meaning of their lives was now possible. Sunday Eucharist retains this importance. It is the weekly celebration of all the newness and hope and fulfillment that God has brought and continues to bring into the world through Jesus the Christ and the Spirit.

The mystery of the divine sacrifice that brings new life has long been at the heart of Catholic spirituality. The Eucharist is an offering to us not only to share life together, but to share together in the very life of God. As the apostle Paul long ago told the church at Corinth:

> *...the Lord Jesus, on the night he was handed over, took bread, and after he had given thanks, broke it and said, "This is my body that is for you. Do this in remembrance of me." In the same way also the cup, after supper, saying, "This cup is the new covenant in my blood. Do this as often as you drink it, in remembrance of me. For as often as you eat this bread and drink this cup, you proclaim the death of the Lord until he comes."*
>
> 1 CORINTHIANS 11:23–26

The Eucharist has elicited deep reverence and awe and given rise to prayers, hymns, and theological treatises.

Among the most cherished of devotional responses to the mystery of the divine presence in the bread and wine is Thomas Aquinas' eucharistic hymn, *Pange Lingua Gloriosa,* originally written for the feast of Corpus Christi or the Body and Blood of Christ. The haunting plain chant melody that accompanies it is heard in churches around the world on Holy Thursday during the procession from the church to the place where the sacrament is kept until Good Friday. The last two stanzas, separately called *Tantum Ergo,* are familiar to those who attend the service of Benediction of the Blessed Sacrament:

Pange, lingua, gloriosi
Corporis mysterium,
Sanguinisque pretiosi,
quem in mundi pretium
fructus ventris generosi
Rex effudit Gentium.

(Sing, my tongue, the Savior's glory,
of His flesh the mystery sing;
of the Blood, all price exceeding,
shed by our immortal King,
destined, for the world's redemption,
from a noble womb to spring.)

Nobis datus, nobis natus
ex intacta Virgine,
et in mundo conversatus,
sparso verbi semine,
sui moras incolatus
miro clausit ordine.

(Of a pure and spotless Virgin
born for us on earth below,
He, as Man, with man conversing,
stayed, the seeds of truth to sow;
then He closed in solemn order
wondrously His life of woe.)

In supremae nocte coenae
recumbens cum fratribus
observata lege plene
cibis in legalibus,
cibum turbae duodenae
se dat suis manibus.

(On the night of that Last Supper,
seated with His chosen band,
He the Pascal victim eating,
first fulfills the Law's command;
then as Food to His Apostles
gives Himself with His own hand.)

Verbum caro, panem verum
verbo carnem efficit:
fitque sanguis Christi merum,
et si sensus deficit,
ad firmandum cor sincerum
sola fides sufficit.

(Word-made-Flesh, the bread of nature
by His word to Flesh He turns;
wine into His Blood He changes;
what though sense no change discerns?
Only be the heart in earnest,
faith her lesson quickly learns.)

Tantum ergo Sacramentum
veneremur cernui:
et antiquum documentum
novo cedat ritui:
praestet fides supplementum
sensuum defectui.

(Down in adoration falling,
Lo! the sacred Host we hail;
Lo! o'er ancient forms departing,
newer rites of grace prevail;
faith for all defects supplying,
where the feeble senses fail.)

Genitori, Genitoque
laus et jubilatio,
salus, honor, virtus quoque
sit et benedictio:
Procedenti ab utroque
compar sit laudatio.

(To the everlasting Father,
and the Son who reigns on high,
with the Holy Ghost proceeding
forth from Each eternally,
be salvation, honor, blessing,
might and endless majesty.)

Amen Alleluia.

PANGE LINGUA GLORIOSI

THE LITURGICAL YEAR

The Church not only provides us the opportunity to pray together at the Eucharist, it also helps us pray through the course of the seasons of the year and the seasons of our lives. Since at least the fourth century, Christians have structured time so that we are temporally immersed in the redemptive mysteries of faith. The two central truths of Christian faith—the incarnation and resurrection—which proclaim that God is with us and that divine Love conquers sin and death, anchor the Christian year. Around these two great mysteries, the Church structures periods of preparation and of expanded celebration. The colors of the liturgical vestments, the decorations on the altar, the mood of the hymnody, the special prayers and ritual gestures all alert us to the particular mystery that we celebrate.

Thus Advent allows us to make straight the highways of our hearts and minds upon which the Lord will travel to us. The banners or drapery in the church are purple or dark blue, signaling the reflective mood of the season. The haunting plain chant, *Veni, veni Emmanuel* ("O Come, O Come Emmanuel"), ushers us into silent sanctuaries. The music is more muted; no alleluias are sung. Instead, we are invited into introspection, asked to prepare our hearts and to consider what is to come. The season of Advent alerts us to the three Comings—past, present, and future—that our faith proclaims: the Incarnation of Christ as a baby born in a manger in Bethlehem two thousand years ago, the ever recurring coming of Christ into each of our hearts, and the

Second Coming of Christ at the end of time. At the onset of the season, we are told of the final judgment, of God's mighty coming at the end of time when all will come before the divine throne. We then hear the prophetic words of the camel-hair clad John the Baptist, crying in the wilderness, "One mightier than I is coming after me" (Mark 1:7). Prepare the way! Finally, with Mary, we attend to the words of the angel Gabriel who announces the astonishing news: a child will be born, and he will be called *Immanuel*, "God is with you." In this season we prepare, we wait, we keep vigil, we ready our hearts for the celebration of God-with-us in the tiny babe in Bethlehem, for the invitation that God extends to each of us, and for the final Coming at the end of time. There is much to say about the liturgical season of Advent, but as an annual and communal spiritual practice, it is beyond compare.

Similarly, Lent prepares us to more truly receive the astonishing message of Easter by following closely in the footsteps of Jesus as he moves toward Jerusalem and enters into the passion and death that will ultimately bring new life. The mood is deeply solemn. We are urged by the season to empty and ready ourselves through penitential practices, fasts, the sacrament of reconciliation, and acts of charity. Often on the Fridays of Lent, the Stations of the Cross are re-enacted. Participants follow in the footsteps of Jesus as he is condemned, takes up his cross, and makes his painful way toward Golgotha. The refrain, "We adore you, O Christ, and we bless you, because by your holy cross, you have redeemed the world," punctuates the ritual action. Lenten Stations of the Cross may take many forms. In some parishes or communities, a Justice Walk is dramatized, with devotees marking the stations at local sites where violence and injustices of contemporary society are visible: battered women's shelters, hostels for the homeless, soup kitchens, immigration centers. Jesus is thus condemned again in the victims of domestic violence, hunger, unemployment, and homelessness. And the hope of resurrection is linked to the hope and action on behalf of a more just world.

Holy Week dramatizes and allows us an even more profound access to the salvation brought by Jesus' own human suffering that not only took place long ago, but which takes place continually in each of our own lives. We travel with Jesus in his last days. Palms waving, we welcome him into Jerusalem with the cheering crowds, but soon the mood darkens. We gather with the disciples for what will be the Last Supper they will share with the one who has so captured their hearts with his vision of the reign of God. Jesus, teacher and friend, foretells his betrayal, delivers his last admonitions, and with the telling gesture of washing his disciples' feet, shows them (and us) how we must love one another as we have been loved. "Do you realize what I have done for you? You call me 'teacher' and 'master,' and rightly so, for indeed I am. If I, therefore, the master and teacher, have washed your feet, you ought to wash one another's feet. I have given you a model to follow, so that as I have done for you, you should also do" (John 13:12–15). Then Jesus retires to the Garden of Gethsemane, begging his friends to keep watch with him. Instead, they (and we with them) fall asleep.

Betrayed by a companion's kiss, Jesus is taken to his inglorious death upon a cross. With Jesus we are scourged, nailed, mocked, and left abandoned to die. The liturgical power of Holy Week sweeps us up in its drama. We become a part of the events, made aware not only of the saving events of the past and the offering of love made on our behalf, but of the extent to which these events have currency today. We are the crucifiers, the onlookers, those who deny him and stay by his side; we are the devastated mother and the shocked disciples, and we are the crucified. We enter into the dynamic of the seasons through the ritual actions of the liturgy, taking them as the template with which to shape and comprehend and transform our lives.

One of the most arresting Holy Week rituals in the United States takes place in New Mexico at the tiny shrine of El Santuario de Chimayo. Thousands of pilgrims head toward the unprepossessing chapel in the hills beyond Santa Fe. Many come on foot from as far away as Albuquerque or Los Alamos, as penitents or because of a vow. Some carry crosses; most do so in solidarity with the one who suffered and died for them. They may have asked for healing for a loved one and promised to walk if a cure was found. They may come simply in gratitude for some grace or as an act of penance. But they come especially in Holy Week, the week in which the mystery of new life emerging from death is experienced once again.

At the crux of the liturgical cycle, at the moment of greatest sorrow, the Church begins its great turning. The solemn Vigil of Easter begins with the singing of the ancient Exsultet, the triumphant proclamation of the Easter faith:

Exsultet iam Angélica turba caelórum:
exsultent divina mystéria:
et pro tanti Regis victória, tuba insonet salutáris.

Rejoice, heavenly powers! Sing, choirs of angels!
Exult, all creation around God's throne!
Jesus Christ, our King, is risen!
Sound the trumpet of salvation!

Gáudeat et tellus tantis irradiáta fulgóribus:
et, aetérni Regis splendóre illustrata,
totius orbis se sentiat amisisse caliginem.

Rejoice, O earth, in shining splendor,
radiant in the brightness of your King!
Christ has conquered! Glory fills you!
Darkness vanishes for ever!

Laetetur et mater Ecclesia,
tanti luminis adornata fulgóribus:
et magnis populórum vócibus haec aula resultet.

Rejoice, O Mother Church! Exult in glory!
The risen Savior shines upon you!
Let this place resound with joy,
echoing the mighty song of all God's people!

Quaprópter astantes vos, fratres carissimi,
ad tam miram huius sancti luminis claritatem,
una mecum, quaeso,
Dei omnipotentis misericórdiam invocate.
Ut, qui me non meis meritis
intra Levitarum numerum dignatus est aggregare,
luminis sui claritatem infundens,
cerei huius laudem implere perficiat.

My dearest friends, standing with me in this holy light,
join me in asking God for mercy,
that he may give his unworthy minister
grace to sing his Easter praises.

Vers. Dóminus vobiscum.

Resp. Et cum spiritu tuo.

Vers. Sursum corda.

Resp. Habemus ad Dóminum.

Vers. Gratias agamus Dómino Deo nostro.

Resp. Dignum et iustum est.

Deacon: The Lord be with you.

People: And also with you.

Deacon: Lift up your hearts.

People: We lift them up to the Lord.

Deacon: Let us give thanks to the Lord our God.

People: It is right to give him thanks and praise.

Vere dignum et iustum est,
invisibilem Deum Patrem omnipotentem
Filiumque eius Unigenitum,
Dóminum nostrum Iesum Christum,
toto cordis ac mentis affectu et vocis ministerio personare.

It is truly right
that with full hearts and minds and voices
we should praise the unseen God,
the all-powerful Father,
and his only Son, our Lord Jesus Christ.

Qui pro nobis aeterno Patri Adae debitum solvit,
et veteris piaculi cautiónem pio cruore detersit.

For Christ has ransomed us with his blood,
and paid for us the price of Adam's sin
to our eternal Father!

Haec sunt enim festa paschalia,
in quibus verus ille Agnus occiditur,
cuius sanguine postes fidelium consecrantur.

This is our passover feast,
when Christ, the true Lamb, is slain,
whose blood consecrates the homes of all believers.

Haec nox est,
in qua primum patres nostros,
filios Israel eductos de Aegypto,
Mare Rubrum sicco vestigio transire fecisti.

This is the night when first you saved our fathers:
you freed the people of Israel from their slavery
and led them dry-shod through the sea.

Haec igitur nox est,
quae peccatórum tenebras columnae illuminatióne purgavit.

This is the night when the pillar of fire
destroyed the darkness of sin!

Haec nox est,
quae hódie per universum mundum in Christo credentes,
a vitiis saeculi et caligine peccatórum segregatos,
reddit gratiae, sóciat sanctitati.

This is the night when Christians everywhere,
washed clean of sin
and freed from all defilement,
are restored to grace and grow together in holiness.

Haec nox est,
in qua, destructis vinculis mortis,
Christus ab inferis victor ascendit.

This is the night when Jesus Christ
broke the chains of death
and rose triumphant from the grave.

Nihil enim nobis nasci prófuit, nisi redimi profuisset.
O mira circa nos tuae pietatis dignatio!
O inaestimabilis dilectio caritatis:
ut servum redimeres, Filium tradidisti!

What good would life have been to us,
had Christ not come as our Redeemer?

Father, how wonderful your care for us!
How boundless your merciful love!
To ransom a slave
you gave away your Son.

O certe necessarium Adae peccatum,
quod Christi morte deletum est!

O felix culpa,
quae talem ac tantum meruit habere Redemptórem!

O happy fault, O necessary sin of Adam,
which gained for us so great a Redeemer!

O vere beata nox,
quae sola meruit scire tempus et horam,
in qua Christus ab inferis resurrexit!

Most blessed of all nights, chosen by God
to see Christ rising from the dead!

Haec nox est, de qua scriptum est:
Et nox sicut dies illuminabitur:
et nox illuminatio mea in deliciis meis.

Of this night scripture says:
"The night will be as clear as day:
it will become my light, my joy."

Huius igitur sanctificatio noctis fugat scelera, culpas lavat:
et reddit innocentiam lapsis et maestis laetitiam.
Fugat ódia, concórdiam parat et curvat imperia.

The power of this holy night
dispels all evil, washes guilt away,
restores lost innocence, brings mourners joy;
it casts out hatred, brings us peace, and humbles
earthly pride.

O vere beata nox,
in qua terrenis caelestia, humanis divina iunguntur!

Night truly blessed when heaven is wedded to earth
and man is reconciled with God!

In huius igitur noctis gratia,
suscipe, sancte Pater,
laudis huius sacrificium vespertinum,
quod tibi in hac cerei oblatióne solemni,
per ministrórum manus de operibus apum,
sacrosancta reddit Ecclesia.

Therefore, heavenly Father, in the joy of this night,
receive our evening sacrifice of praise,
your Church's solemn offering.

Sed iam columnae huius praecónia nóvimus,
quam in honórem Dei rutilans ignis accendit.

Accept this Easter candle,
a flame divided but undimmed,
a pillar of fire that glows to the honor of God.

Oramus ergo te, Dómine:
ut cereus iste in honórem tui nóminis consecratus,
ad noctis huius caliginem destruendam,
indeficiens perseveret.

Et in odórem suavitatis acceptus,
supernis luminaribus misceatur.

Let it mingle with the lights of heaven
and continue bravely burning
to dispel the darkness of this night!

Flammas eius lucifer matutinus inveniat:
Ille, inquam, lucifer, qui nescit occasum.
Christus Filius tuus,
qui, regressus ab inferis, humano generi serenus illuxit,
et vivit et regnat in saecula saeculorum.

May the morning Star which never sets find this flame
still burning:
Christ, that Morning Star,
who came back from the dead,
and shed his peaceful light on all mankind,
your Son who lives and reigns for ever and ever.
Amen.

We are recipients of the long story of salvation history and
are led with the grieving women to the edge of the empty
tomb, where we too will gaze in astonishment at what we
find there. Easter Sunday, with its astounding revelation of
the empty tomb, is followed by an entire fifty-day season in
which the implications of that mystery unfold. With trumpets
and lilies, the Church ablaze with gold and white vestments
and voices singing Alleluias, we renew our baptismal vows,
promising to live into the fullness of the mysteries we have
been reliving during the Church year. We share at this time
in the story of Jesus' first appearances to the grieving disciples
and participate in the birth of the fledging church. Then,
in the long weeks of Ordinary Time, the Church encourages us to reflect on the life and ministry of Christ. We hear
again the stories of his healings; we ponder the parables of

the kingdom; we find ourselves confronted by the witness of his saving works. We are invited to walk with him. Each Sunday of the church year, we enter again into the passion and resurrection, savor the Easter revelation, and celebrate God's saving gift.

Catholic spiritual traditions are saturated with these varied dynamics of the liturgical year, its feasts and fasts, and its particular rhythms. This is our common heritage, the story that makes us who we are as a people and as individuals. For it is not only in the Church's dramatic liturgy that we participate in the Christ event. These liturgical seasons are more intimately understood as the essential backdrop against which our personal spiritual dramas unfold. They are the loom upon which our lives are woven into the life of Christ.

DAILY COMMON PRAYER: LITURGY OF THE HOURS

As important as the observance of the Lord's day (Sunday), which celebrates the resurrection, has become over the years, the fact is that the earliest Christians were not always able to observe this together: Sunday was a work day. It was only gradually, as the Roman Empire was Christianized, that an acknowledged common day off came into being. But from the beginning, Christians prayed together each day. Morning and evening, before and after work, gatherings took place. Prayer that punctuates the day had been a practice within the Jewish community from which Christianity was born. It was tradition for Jewish men to formally acknowledge the presence of the Divine in the morning, afternoon, and evening. As the Christian community developed, the idea of daily prayer continued.

The Church flourished and monastic communities were established, and daily prayer became the backbone of the life of these praying communities of women or men. The daily office or the Liturgy of the Hours, which is found in the Roman Breviary, allows for an intensive immersion in the common prayer of the Church. It is prayed throughout the day all over the world. It is prayed by monks, priests, brothers, and many other apostolic religious communities, as well as by lay people who wish to sanctify time each day. The full office consists of seven "hours" of prayer (hymns, psalms, and readings) that conform loosely to the hours of the day: Office of Readings, Morning Prayer, Mid-morning/Midday/Mid-afternoon Prayer (often combined), Evening Prayer, and Night Prayer. Praying the Liturgy of the Hours, in long or short form, is both a private act and a deeply communal one, since when praying the assigned prayers of the day or week, we are praying with all those, near or far, who also do so.

Some of the most beautiful and memorable images that have shaped the Catholic imagination over the centuries come from the readings that punctuate the daily prayers, for example, Psalm 63: "O God, you are my God—for you I long! For you my body yearns; for you my soul thirsts, Like a land parched, lifeless, and without water." Psalm141 is often sung at evening prayer: "Let my prayer be incense before you; my uplifted hands an evening sacrifice." Psalm 139 reads: O Lord, you have probed me, you know me: you know when I sit and stand; you understand my thoughts from afar."

Likewise, the great biblical canticles found in the Gospel of Luke are sung during the daily prayers. In the morning office, the astonishing dawn of redemption prophesied by Zechariah is once again proclaimed by all: "And you, child, will be called prophet of the Most High, for you will go before the Lord to prepare his ways, to give his people knowledge of salvation, the forgiveness of their sins" (Luke 1:76–77). This canticle is known by its traditional title, the Benedictus. Mary's fulsome song of praise, her Magnificat, rings out at vespers or evening prayer: "My soul proclaims the greatness of the Lord; my spirit rejoices in God my savior" (Luke 1:46–47). Each day closes gently with the canticle, *Nunc Dimittis*, intoned by the aged priest Simeon, as he holds the newborn Christ Child: "Now master, you may let your servant go in peace, according to your word, for my eyes have seen your salvation…" (Luke 2:29–30). These canticles echo across the centuries and across the globe as Catholics pray into the mystery of God's mercy.

Praying the Liturgy of the Hours sanctifies time. It creates, as it were, a lattice work through which the sense of another sort of time permeates our experience. *Chronos*, or clock time, is often perceived as moving quickly, as getting away from us. *Chronos* is chronological. We never seem to have enough of it. We are hurried. Time seems to age us. It takes things away. In contrast, *Kairos* is God's time. It is the appointed time in the purpose of God, the time in which God acts. We experience *Kairos* as eternity intersects with chronological time. God's time is spacious, generative, life-giving, restorative. Praying at any time provides us access to God's time, but praying the offices does so daily and rhythmically.

4. The Communion of Saints

During each eucharistic liturgy, as the community joins to pray with the priest over the gifts that have been prepared, the saints are invoked: "Now let us pray with all the angels and saints." This proclamation expresses the insight, fundamental to the Catholic imagination, that we are not alone in our prayer. Not only are we joined together with all those who are presently praying, but we are part of a communion that spans time and space.

The Church is more than the people gathered in the pews, more than the priests, deacons, and bishops who officiate. The Church consists of those who are presently alive walking the path of faith, those who have died and are in the process of being purified for the final Coming of Christ, and those who are already with God. These last, the saints, including the martyrs and those whose lives have been closely conformed to Christ's life, witness for us the many ways that the inexhaustible holiness of Christ has been expressed throughout the centuries. They are also present to us, available as intercessors. Their intimacy with God allows us intimacy as well.

The Dogmatic Constitution on the Church (*Lumen Gentium*) names those of us who are still engaged in the walk of faith on earth "the pilgrim church." This includes institutions, sacramental rituals, and persons. "All of us…in varying degrees and in different ways, share in the same love of God and our neighbor, and we all sing the same hymn of glory to God. All, indeed, who are of Christ and who have his Spirit form one church and in Christ are joined together" (*LG* 49). In the Mystical Body of which Christ is head, the pilgrim church is united with the saints and with all those who have died in Christ.

Another traditional way to talk about our communion with the saints is to identify the Church in its three aspects: the "church militant," or those who, on earth, continue to walk the path; the "church suffering," or the dead in purgatory; and the "church triumphant," or those holy ones who have died and are presently with God. Either way one describes this, the fact is that for Catholics, time and space are not restrictive. Our deeper lives extend beyond the confines of our geographical location, our historical moment, and our personal relationships and experiences. Our deeper lives are immense and are connected in profound ways to the lives of those who go before us.

If, as has been suggested, Catholic spirituality is about being more and more conformed to Christ, albeit in countless manners and ways, then those persons who have seemed to their contemporaries to embody the truth of the Gospel, who have been signs of God's kingdom, are important people. They are the ones who manifest, or make visible, the fullness of life that Jesus preached. If one takes a contemporary example, Mother Teresa of Calcutta, one finds that her life inspired others. Spontaneously, she was named a living saint. Her ministry to the dying in the streets of Calcutta, as well as the Missionaries of Charity, the religious community she founded to tend to the forgotten and abandoned in urban centers around the globe, spoke to the age in which she lived.

This is the Gospel in action that compelled her admirers to comment.

Of course, being officially named a saint by the Church is a more thorough and lengthy process than simply being identified by one's contemporaries as such. But the process starts there, and that is an important fact. True saints are not conformed to Christ for their own glorification or even their own salvation. They are transparent, visible signs of the Spirit's work, precisely for others. They are witnesses to the goodness of God, to the beauty of the kingdom, to the truth of the Gospel. The documents of Vatican II reaffirm this ancient intuition of the communion of saints. Those who toil and love and live as all people, "sharing our humanity," become for us the "image of Christ." In them and through their living example, we know God's presence with us on earth. They are "the face of God"; when we strive to live by their example, we are the face of God for one another. In this way, the words "your will be done on earth as in heaven" find a way into our own reality. As the Dogmatic Constitution on the Church clearly states, the "truth of the Gospel" is lived in the saints and in the daily life of the pilgrim church (*LG* 50).

Threaded throughout the Church year is the cycle of celebrations of saints' feasts. In fact, the earliest calendar that Christians kept was a memorial of the deaths of the martyrs, celebrations that made note of their "second births" into eternal life. Through the cycles of the liturgical seasons and saints' feasts, Catholics are immersed in the mysteries of faith and made aware of the holy ones who are their spiritual companions and to whom they may come for inspiration, encouragement, and intercession.

THE VIRGIN MARY

Chief among those who have gone before us and who model the life of faith is Mary, the Mother of Jesus. Among the many titles that those who love and honor her have bestowed on her over the years is the title, Queen of Saints. What that might mean will concern us shortly. But she has many other titles as well, and these other aspects of her gracious presence are important in the history and practice of Catholic spirituality.

Mary is mother. She is the human mother of Jesus, and as such, has a special relationship with her Son. Catholic spiritual traditions leave us a rich legacy of reflection on Mary as a human mother. We hear of her in the Scriptures read at the liturgy. In paintings, illustrations, woodcuts, statuary, stained glass, poetry, prayers, and hymns we experience her receiving the startling news of her impending pregnancy, hurrying to visit her elderly cousin who also finds herself with child, hovering at the crib of her newborn child, searching in the Temple for her lost adolescent son, worrying about the wine at a wedding they attend together, grieving as her Son passes by on his way to his execution on Calvary, and sorrowing at the foot of the cross.

Her story comes to us from Scripture, but also through the Church's unfolding tradition. And it is that story that reveals the life that expands beyond her role as Mother of Jesus. Tradition tells of her immaculate conception in the womb of her mother, Anne, her childhood with devout parents, Joachim and Anne, her youthful preparation to be the Mother of the Savior, her marriage to Joseph, the loving domestic life of her little family, her joyful meeting with her risen Son, her assumption into heaven at death and her esteemed place now with God. Some parts of the story have become formally enshrined as definitive teachings of the faith; some still function mainly in popular devotion. But Mary's story is a significant one for Catholic spirituality.

She is Mother of Jesus, but she also fulfills a maternal role for the whole Church. The Litany of Loreto, that great Marian prayer that gained importance in the early modern period, describes some of the ways in which Mary's motherhood is sensed. She is named Mother of divine grace, Mother most pure, Mother most chaste, Mother inviolate, Mother unde-filed, Mother most amiable, Mother most admirable, Mother of good Counsel. She is the maternal one whose tender care ministers to us, whose protective mantle enfolds us. She is Mother of the Church; her presence at Pentecost, recorded in Scripture (Acts 2), marks her as present at the birth of the new Christian community. With the Apostles, she receives the in-flowing rush of the Spirit that is to animate the Church over the centuries. Often she has been depicted in iconography with her long protective mantle sheltering a huddled group of petitioners like a mother hen sheltering her chicks.

Yet her maternity goes beyond that of a human mother or even a mother of the faithful. Early on, the Church of-ficially recognized that she was *Theotokos* or "God-bearer." In the Catholic West, this appellation has been translated as "Mother of God." Here her cosmic role in the mystery of salvation is underscored. Mary is not simply the biological mother of the human Jesus, she is the vessel in which the divine Christ is offered to the world. She is the throne upon which divine Wisdom seats himself.

Closely related to her maternal presence is Mary's role as patroness and protector. Many Catholic communities look to her as the one who guides and shelters them in a special manner. Religious communities of all sorts have taken her as their model and patron. The worldwide Cistercian monastic family is under Mary's protection, and most individual monasteries bear her name. Perhaps the most famous monastery of the Cistercians of the Strict Observance (known as the Trappists) is the Abbey of Our Lady of Gethsemani in Kentucky. It was from that abbey that mid-twentieth century spiritual leader Thomas Merton wrote his popular books and kept a correspondence with some of the world's most influential spiritual figures. Innumerable other Catholic religious communities, parishes, groups, and organizations take Mary as patroness.

The Catholic churches of Latin America and the Caribbean each have their own image of Mary who is honored as patroness of their respective countries. As Catholics from these countries have established themselves in North America over long periods, these Marian images have become ever-present throughout churches in the United States:

- Our Lady of Charity of El Cobre (*Nuestra Señora del la Caridad del Cobre*), patroness of Cuba, is honored especially in Florida, where a shrine has been built in her honor. Often she is depicted according to the legend of her image's origin, poised above a small boat that carries the three "Juans" who, in 1600, are said to have discovered a miraculously dry statue of her in the sea after a ferocious storm.

- *La Altagracia*, the Virgin who holds the Dominican Republic close in her heart, is visible in churches all over New York, where the Dominican population is concentrated. The blue-robed Altagracia, her head encircled by stars, gazes tenderly at the newborn child lying before her.

- Similarly, in the Pico Union district of Los Angeles, where many Catholics from Central Americans live, you will find images of the elegant white-gowned Salvadoran *Nuestra Señora de la Paz*, holding a palm leaf aloft, and Honduras' *Nuestra Señora de Suyapa*, surrounded by two semicircles of silver rays, her small dark hands clasped in prayer.

- Most notably, it is Our Lady of Guadalupe, the patroness, indeed the empress, of the Americas, that is the most uniquely identifiable image of the Virgin in the United States. The image is of Mexican origin and still compels special devotion among Mexican Americans, but Guadalupe stands proudly as a rich, complex symbol of the history and hope of Catholicism in what was once seen from Europe as the New World. Her story is a familiar one, stemming from the early days of Spanish conquest of Aztec Mexico. The beloved legend, relayed

here in the words found on the "Mary Page" sponsored
by the Marianist Order, reads this way:

Greatly astonished, the Franciscan bishop of Mexico,
Fray Juan de Zumarraga, contemplates the fresh
roses of Castille that sprinkle with colors the floor
of his Episcopal palace. Tears run down his cheeks
as he recognizes the beautiful image that has just
appeared on the rough cloth that [the poor peas-
ant] Juan Diego has unfolded in his presence. It is
Tuesday, December 12, 1531, scarcely ten years after
the conquest of Mexico, and the Mother of God has
come to the defeated Indians to "show and give" all
her "love and compassion, help and defense, because
I am your merciful mother." For four days the Virgin
has told her wishes to Juan Diego, talking to him
in *nahualtl*, his own tongue....[T]he *nahualtl* word
sounded to the Spanish friars like *Guadalupe*, relating
the Tepeyac apparition with the beloved title which
the conquistadores venerated in [Spain].

"THE MARY PAGE," THE MARIAN LIBRARY
INTERNATIONAL MARIAN RESEARCH INSTITUTE

The figure of the Virgin that Juan Diego encountered on the
hill of Tepayac was clothed in royal symbols familiar in Aztec
iconography, as well as symbols reminiscent of the "woman
clothed with the sun" in the biblical Book of Revelation, a
female figure identified with the eschatological fulfillment
of creation. There is much more that might and should be

said about Guadalupe, some of which will be treated shortly, but it is important to note that Guadalupe's patronage has extended widely since she was first venerated in Mexico at the dawn of the sixteenth century. Pope Pius X made the Guadalupana patroness of all Latin American countries in 1910. Pius XI extended her patronage to the Philippines in 1935. Pius XII, in 1945, called her "Empress of the Americas," and John XXIII described her as the "celestial missionary of the New World" and "Mother of the Americas." Pope John Paul II saw in her not only the "Mother of the Church in Latin America," but also the "Star of Evangelization" of the whole subcontinent. Her patronage is presently seen to extend to the entire hemisphere.

The eschatological aspects of the Guadalupe image suggest that there is another, most significant dimension of Marian devotion that is important for Catholic spirituality. Over the centuries and in a variety of ways, Mary has been perceived as a model of a transformed humanity. She is the new creation, the promise of God fulfilled.

In the middle ages, contemplative monks (those explorers of intimacy with the Divine in prayer) meditated on Mary at the moment of the annunciation when the angel Gabriel came to her and told her she would be bear a child. This passage, of course, is theologically central to the faith: it is the prelude to the Incarnation, to God becoming human, to the birth of Jesus, God-with-us. But for the contemplatives, this passage had layers of meaning, a central one being about how we, as humans, are to receive the divine Spirit.

We are to be like Mary, welcoming God's gentle initiative.

We are, in the words of twelfth century Cistercian Guerric of Igny, "Mothers of God." In a sermon preached to members of his own monastic community, Guerric cautioned that the divine Word, which has been implanted in our hearts, must be brought to birth in our lives. The dangers of not caring for that Word, of letting it be stillborn, are real. Guerric's image is perhaps startling to contemporary sensibilities, but it recalls the scriptural image (Matthew 13) of seeds falling on hard, rocky, thorny, or good soil, only the last of which bore fruit. For Guerric and for the contemplative tradition, Mary is the contemplative human person, the one who prepares her or himself to bring the Word to birth in her or his own flesh.

In the spiritual traditions, the paradox of Mary's motherhood and her virginity speak to the deep mystery revealed in Guerric's symbolism, a symbolism that others utilized as well. The immaculate conception (Mary's exemption from the effects of original sin at the time of her conception in Anne's womb) and the virgin birth (the virginal conception of Jesus), like the annunciation, have theological and salvific import but can also be, and have often been, read as spiritual truths applicable to all Christians. The person who will be most fruitful will be pure of heart; will know God to be at the center of life; will have the capacity to sort through the conflicting demands of society, culture, family, and even a heart pulled in many directions, to discover the plumb line that is God. Mary, thus oriented, is a model for all persons. She is the new creation, the new person who realizes the promises to which we are all heir.

This astonishing thought, that we each are called to carry Christ into the world, that we are all destined to be new creations, is at the root of Marian spirituality. Mary is not only her own unique person (the Church affirms this in the teachings about her immaculate conception and her assumption) but she represents a human life transformed. She is newness personified. She is not only admirable, but imitable. Over the centuries this intuition has taken many forms. Some of these forms, in prayers, treatises and hymnody, are familiar. Others, less familiar, are none the less fresh and engaging, as is this Marian meditation by Juana Inés de la Cruz, a seventeenth century Hieronymite nun in colonial Mexico. The association with birds comes from the fact that the well-known Latin address to the Virgin, *Ave* ("hail"), is also the Spanish word for bird:

> Ave, ave, Reina de las aves! Hail, hail, Queen of the birds! Hail, bird crowned and soaring above all creatures! Ave gratia plena! (Luke 1:28). As the archangel St. Gabriel saluted you with this name, so we invoke you with the same! Teach us, divine bird, so that our affections take flight, Teach us like the eagle who teaches her chicks by flying above them. Inspire the flight of our contemplation so that we may drink in the rays of the sun of justice and protect us beneath your wings from the infernal serpent. Grant that in the secure nest of your fervent devotion and under the sovereign refuge of your maternal vigilance, we may pass through the perils and troubles of this life

to fly to the heights of glory in your company. There
we will enjoy the clear light of the Lord, the beatific
vision, which we hope to possess in your company
for all eternity.

JUANA INÉS DE LA CRUZ: SELECTED WRITINGS

On the other side of the Atlantic, in seventeenth century
Europe, when there was much interest in the interior experiences of Jesus and those who followed and lived with him,
the spiritual focus was on the qualities of Mary's heart. Saint
Jean Eudes, who founded the Eudists and the Congregation
of Our Lady of Charity in France, wrote glowingly of the
qualities of her heart and its intimate connection to the heart
of her Son. This oneness of hearts, this deep cleaving to the
interior truth of the person at once human and divine, was
what all human beings are meant to do.

A generation before Eudes, Savoyard Saint Francis de Sales
painted a word-picture of a world of conjoined divine-human
hearts linked by the gentle, humble heart of the crucified Jesus
(Matthew 11:29–30), the human heart that beat perfectly in
rhythm with God's. God's intent or heart-longing for each
person was that they would be what they were created to be,
lovers with hearts aligned to the divine heart. Each needed to
let Jesus live in the heart, to have a heart transformed. Such
a heart enshrined the little, relational virtues like humility,
gentleness, patience, kindness, and simplicity. It was Mary
who did this most gracefully. For de Sales, Mary conceived
Christ first in her heart, well before he was conceived in her
womb. Because God had preserved her from the effects of sin

at the moment of her conception, she was the human being who was truly free to love fully, with all the expansiveness of which human beings are capable. She could truly "live Jesus." Thus Francis de Sales taught that while she may have enjoyed special privileges, she was still the human model of the Spirit-filled Christian life. She grew in grace, and thus her life was morally imitable as well as worthy of special veneration. Especially was she the model for the religious life.

More contemporarily, Mary in her guise as Our Lady of Guadalupe speaks clearly of the new creation in a fresh way. American Latino theologian Virgil Elizondo speaks rapturously of her in this manner:

> At the very center of the Guadalupe image is the Nahuatl glyph that appears at the center of the old Aztec representation of the cosmos….[that] indicates that the previous ages…of the world have been assumed and a new one is about to begin….
>
> The image is both the sign and the announcement of the truly new creation of the Americas—not a "new" world that would simply rebuild the old ways of conquest, greed, avarice, subjugation, and wars in a new space, but a new world that would be authentically new because of its inclusion of all the peoples of all the Americas as children of the one Mother…. In asking for a temple where she can give all her love and compassion, the Lady is in effect speaking about the reign of God that was the core of the life and message of Jesus. Guadalupe is thus a good Nahuatl

translation of the New Testament reality of the reign
of God as revealed by Jesus.

GUADALUPE, MOTHER OF THE NEW CREATION

Mary points in fact to a world transformed into God's promised kingdom, a reign of justice and peace where all persons will thrive as God intends.

Other contemporary theologians and spiritual writers have likewise viewed Mary as a sign of the new creation in the sense that she is a human woman to be emulated because she delved deep into her own creative capacity and followed God, rather than following human convention or societal norms. Rejecting what is expected of her and following the radical invitation of God to follow Jesus, even to the foot of the cross, underscores Mary's role as a disciple. Each Christian is similarly asked to act on behalf of the promised kingdom, to invite a transformed world where, to quote Jesus' own words uttered at the inauguration of his ministry, "...he has anointed me to bring glad tidings to the poor...sent me to proclaim liberty to captives and recovery of sight to the blind, to let the oppressed go free and to proclaim a year acceptable to the Lord" (Luke 4:18–19).

SAINTS AS MODELS AND INTERCESSORS

As with Mary, Queen of Saints, Catholics have had varied relationships with that great cloud of witnesses, the saints. Saints can serve as models and inspiration to us as to how we might be formed in the divine image and likeness. We may find our conscience pricked as we learn of Saint Mother Frances Cabrini, who traveled from her Italian homeland to work on behalf of orphans and the immigrant poor in nineteenth-century New York. Or we may feel called to pastoral ministry, inspired by the witness of Blessed Samuel Mazzuchelli, a Dominican priest who is remembered throughout the Mississippi River Valley and in the Great Lakes region for establishing parish communities, designing and building churches and civic buildings, and founding the Sinsinawa Dominican Sisters. Mazzuchelli's commitment to justice for the oppressed, to education, and to responsible civic participation are seen as relevant values for our time. We may find inspiration in the spiritual writings of Saint Thérèse of Lisieux, the "Little Flower," or be drawn by the witness of Saint Francis of Assisi and his deep reverence for the created world.

But Catholics may also venerate the saints as intercessors. Scholar Lawrence Cunningham has described saints as either imitable or unimitable. In other words, they may inspire us to change our lives, or we may look to them as powerful advocates who intercede for us with God. Much Catholic devotion to the saints is an affirmation of our sense that we are surrounded and upheld by these compassionate and powerful patrons and protectors. We even specify the appropriateness of a given saint's patronage.

Saint Joseph, who taught Jesus his trade, is patron of carpenters. Saint Helen, reputed to have traveled to the holy land and unearthed a fragment of the true cross, is patron of archeologists, while Joan of Arc is patron of members of the military. We turn to Saint Monica, who prayed so earnestly for her son Augustine as he teetered on the brink of conversion, as patron of parents of troubled children. And we look to Saint Bernadette Soubirous, whose chronic asthma was cured at the spring at Lourdes, when we ask for healing for those suffering from that disease. All our prayer and our worship is ultimately directed to God as Father, Son, and Holy Spirit, the One who creates, redeems, and sanctifies. But we can and do venerate Mary and the saints. They are, in a sense, our extended family in the faith. They are intimately united with God, may pray with us, plead for us, and advocate for us.

The intervention of saints on our behalf has been the sense of the Church since earliest times. Saint Jerome, the fifth century biblical translator, affirmed "...if the Apostles and martyrs while still in the body can pray for others, when they ought still to be anxious for themselves, how much more must they do so when once they have won their crowns, overcome, and triumphed?" (*Against Vigilantius*). The intuition here is again that of a common life, a shared life of spiritual kinship in Christ, a kinship that transcends time and space, culture, language, gender, and class.

This very Catholic sensibility of a common life underlies the Church's process of choosing saints. The process, as has been suggested, was originally an organic one. Early Christians spontaneously held up compatriots through whom they felt the presence of the Divine. Saints were those recognized in the community as manifesting holiness. They were memorialized on the first Christian calendars. The Church, over the centuries, has arrived at a formal process of designating saints. But it began with ordinary people honoring their local holy people. What developed then were a huge number of local cults. Eventually, as Rome began more and more to exercise influence over the rest of western Europe, a centralized calendar was developed and, as the liturgical rites of Rome became dominant, the Roman calendar spread. But it was tricky to know exactly who the locally venerated men and women were. Sometimes legends grew up around fictitious figures. Sometimes a local wonder worker would gain notoriety when he was hardly an example of Christian virtue. The need for oversight became obvious. By the thirteenth century, the formal process of designating saintly figures for universal veneration was reserved to the papacy.

During the Catholic Reformation of the sixteenth and early seventeenth centuries, two concerns about canonization emerged. First, abuses needed to be addressed. A group of scholars known as the Bolandists were assigned to review the archives of saints' lives and, using new methods of historical analysis, determine the authenticity and validity of the many holy figures that had accumulated in the past. Second, new legislation was drawn up governing the process itself. A sufficient time had to elapse after the death of a person who might be considered a candidate for the title of saint. Two processes were developed, one for beatification (locally venerated with the title, "Blessed") and one for canonization (enrolled on the universal calendar).

Eighteenth century reforms required that a dossier for a prospective saint be sent to Rome for scrutiny where a trail-like procedure took place. A candidate was assigned a postulator who was opposed by a defender of the faith (devil's advocate), and the two engaged in legal battle over the worthiness of the candidate. Some of the criteria included the exercise of heroic virtue, orthodoxy and influence of teachings and extent writings, and exceptional witness to the power of Christ, attested to by those who knew the candidate or who claimed that a miracle had been obtained through intercession after the candidate's death. The process was further streamlined under the pontificate of John Paul II. The late pontiff hoped to increase the geographical and vocational diversity of the calendar of saints in order to provide familiar and accessible models of holiness for the global Church. When a person is memorialized on the sanctoral cycle (calendar of saints), he or she becomes a visible part of the universal story of God's mercy and goodness that extends across time into the furthest reaches of the world.

Although to most believers the saints are as familiar as relatives, it has sometimes been asserted that Catholics are idolatrous because they seem to worship the saints. Certainly, many Catholic churches, especially those of traditional design, are filled with vivid images of the holy ones. But in fact, this is an inaccurate charge. Catholics do not worship the saints; we worship only God. One of the most ancient disputes in Christianity, argued again and again, has been over the use of images. As far back as the eighth century, feuds broke out between those who opposed the use of imagery (the iconclasts) and those who promoted it (the icondules). In the ensuing controversy, idols were distinguished from icons. The former were worshiped in the pagan world, while later, the icons were only honored as vehicles to go beyond the image to the reality behind it. The affirmation of icon veneration rested on the doctrine of the Incarnation. If God took on flesh in Jesus the Christ, it followed that any medium of the created order could potentially reveal the Divine, if not in quite the same way, nevertheless in a real sense. Just as the full light of the sun was experienced in limited ways through its rays, so the uncreated light of God, the divine essence, could be made visible as created energies in the created world. Icons thus were windows on an eternal reality. Although these ideas were to become most important in Eastern Orthodox Christianity, they have implications for the Catholic world and its veneration of saints. During these controversies, a careful distinction between veneration and worship was developed. Veneration or honor is what we give to the saints. Worship is reserved for God. Thus when we pray with the saints, we are joining their prayers to God. In and through them, we may view and share in the transformed life, a life suffused with divine light, a Christic life.

Saints are our companions, our advocates, our friends, our patrons and protectors, those who both inspire and challenge us to live into the promises to which we are all called. The holiness to which the saints witness belongs to all of us as members of the Mystical Body of Christ. The proximity of the liturgical solemnities of All Saints on November first and All Souls on November second makes this eminently clear. We all share in the holiness of Christ through our baptisms, and through the Spirit, we can be drawn, with the saints we memorialize, more deeply into the fullness of life. When Catholics of Mexican origin hold festive celebrations at the graves of the departed on the Dia de los Muertos (Day of the

Dead) or All Souls day, they are affirming this truth: our small lives transcend time and space, and we all are somehow present to one another in the communion of Saints.

THE CATHOLIC IMAGINATION

In all that we have so far said about the Mystical Body, the intertwined branches of that great, sustaining vine, we have stressed our common life. In our common Scriptures, our Eucharistic liturgy, the rhythms of the liturgical year, our daily prayer, our cleaving to Christ, our kinship with Mary, and the communion of saints to which we belong, we are indeed one—albeit with many parts, variations, historical, and cultural particularities and personal uniqueness.

Clearly much more could be said about the Church, its structure, doctrines, governance, and development from historical and theological perspectives. But it is the reality of this common life that is central where spirituality is concerned. It has been claimed that there is a distinctive "Catholic imagination," a habit of heart and perception that is a result of our common life together. In the term "imagination," fantasy or unreality is not implied. Rather, an imagination is a lens, a way of seeing, a perspective that shapes our actions and sense of the world. The Catholic imagination could be said to have many features, but for our purposes here, three elements might be highlighted. That imagination is Trinitarian, sacramental, and attuned to both paradox and particulars. Such an imagination shapes much of the spiritual life of Catholics today, as well as in the past.

At the core of the Christian intuition about the cosmic

scheme of things is the affirmation of a triune God: Father, Son, and Holy Spirit. During most eucharistic liturgies, this affirmation is recited in the form of the Nicene Creed:

> We believe in one God,
> The Father, the Almighty,
> Maker of heaven and earth,
> Of all that is seen and unseen.
> We believe in one Lord, Jesus Christ,
> the only son of God,
> eternally begotten of the Father,
> God from God, Light from Light,
> true God from true God,
> begotten not made, one in Being with the Father.
> Through him all things were made.
> For us men and for our salvation
>   he came down from heaven;
> by the power of the Holy Spirit
> he was born of the Virgin Mary, and became man.
> For our sake he was crucified under Pontius Pilate;
> He suffered died and was buried.
> On the third day he arose again
> in fulfillment of the Scriptures;
>   he ascended into heaven
> and is seated at the right hand of the Father.
> He will come again to judge the living and the dead
> and his kingdom will have no end.

We believe in the Holy Spirit, the Lord, the giver of life,
who proceeds from the Father and the Son.
With the Father and the Son he is worshipped
   and glorified.
He has spoken through the prophets.
We believe in one holy, catholic and apostolic Church.
We acknowledge one baptism
   for the forgiveness of sins.
We look for the resurrection of the dead
and the life of the world to come. Amen.

The precision and nuance of this central profession of faith took centuries for the early Church community to hammer out, and a thorough explication of this creed could and has warranted the many erudite tombs written about it. Parenthetically, it should be noted that a creed need not be seen as a rigid, fixed set of ideas, but rather as a creative space in which to explore the depth, width, height and breadth of the vision, the imagined reality that is set forth there. Thus the Creed as formulated at Nicaea is such a space in which Catholics learn to find meaning in the world. Here, we will make only several points germane to the Catholic imagination and the spirituality.

First, this creed is an invitation to entrustment. When we proclaim, "We believe," we use the preposition "in" not "that." Certainly our consent to the propositions contained here is assumed. But more deeply than that, we say we believe in these things. We thus affirm that these mysteries of which we speak are a sort of vessel that can carry us over whatever rough waters might besiege us. They are a star that can guide in the dark of night. They are a path that leads to fullness of life. This is not to say that the Catholic Church in its very human expressions—its members, its leaders, its structures, and its daily actions—is utterly perfected or that every action performed by any member is always directly an expression of the divine will. Only a brief encounter with the struggling people of God will believe that. The Dogmatic Constitution on the Church after all reminds us that we are a pilgrim people, very much in progress and on the way. Nevertheless, the mysteries carried by the fallible body are trustworthy. They are themselves the path, the star, the vessel in which we can believe.

One of the most important aspects of these mysteries is the Trinitarian one. For all that might be carefully said about how to best comprehend the relationship between the three Persons and the fact of the triune God, in terms of spirituality, it is the fact that God is known to us as a relationship that is important. Saint Augustine first used the language of love to describe the very nature of God's own self—the Father, Son, and Spirit dynamically interconnected in mutually self-giving love—and Christian thinkers and contemplatives have plumbed that insight since. What does it mean for us that God's own self is relational? That God is known to us as giver, gift and gifting: the Father giving the Son, the Son given to us, the Spirit animating the gift-giving in each and all of us? If we are made in the divine image and likeness, then we too are essentially made to love and be loved. We have stressed in these pages that Catholic spirituality is about communion, common life, shared identity as the Body of Christ. This is directly related to the Trinitarian intuition of our faith. We are not only one with each other in the Body, we and the Body itself participate in the very life of the Triune God as we learn to love God, appreciate God's gracious generosity, follow Christ, and, prompted by the Spirit, love one another well.

The Catholic Trinitarian imagination encoded in the Creed not only involves sensitivity to our common life, but to the relational dynamics of that life. Love is not a concept, but active and alive. It is generative and creative. It gives life, excites hope, and initiates healing. Love does not exist for itself, but for the whole. One way this imagination expresses itself in the contemporary context is in the focus on the common good that underlies much of the Catholic social teaching tradition. This tradition has its roots in the common life and evangelism of the first Christian communities, but comes to its modern and specific expression beginning in the late nineteenth century. Pope Leo XIII's social encyclical, *Rerum Novarum*, stands at the head of a host of ecclesial statements on the social order.

Representative of the spirit of the social teaching tradition alive in the twentieth century is an excerpt from one of Pope John XXIII's devotional reflections:

> It is said that the primary exercise of charity is to honor justice and act accordingly, to give every man his due, not to deny the worker his just reward, to provide for our brothers' needs and also, if need

arises, and at the cost of any personal sacrifice, to fight for justice. But charity to the poor, according to the Gospel commandment, must never lose its distinctive role of preceding, accompanying, inspiring, and completing the work of justice.

Even after the much desired triumph of social justice there will always remain a wide margin for charity to the poor, for our Lord said: "You always have the poor with you."

POPE JOHN XXIII: ESSENTIAL WRITINGS

We are responsible for stewarding God's world in a way so that each person can have the basic means to flourish and develop the gifts that God has bestowed.

The social teaching tradition stresses that from a Catholic perspective, any decisions made, whether they be economic, political, social, or spiritual, should be made with the common good in mind. If we have resources and wealth, we must not only share our excess with those who are in need, we must pursue policies that level the playing field between us. We are not put here simply to amass goods, spiritual or material, for ourselves, our families, or even our nations. The sense of a common good, of love poured out on behalf of others, is intrinsic to the Catholic imagination. It ultimately leads back to the relational, Trinitarian, way in which we understand God's self.

Similarly, the Catholic imagination is sacramental. The sacraments, those seven channels of grace by which we receive spiritual life, nourish us and encourage us to grow in grace. The Nicene Creed clearly connects the sacramental life of the Church to the self-giving of the triune God. But this in turn is based on the more general sacramental intuition: the visible can be the medium through which the invisible is encountered. In other words, the entire material world can be the place of the meeting of human and divine. Of course, this is the basic truth of the Incarnation, that God became human in Jesus the Christ, who became, to use Saint Catherine of Siena's expression, the bridge between the two realities, eternal and temporal. In the Catholic imagination, the visible world is opaque, so that to go to God, we do not leapfrog the living or the particular or the objective reality in which we find ourselves. Rather, we discover the Divine in the world all around us.

We have seen how this sacramental sense of things can extend to visual images of the saints or icons of the heavenly reality. It also applies to our Catholic sensibility about saints themselves. We say we can actually see the works of grace shining through the light-filled lives of holy persons, either those recognized through canonization or hidden from public view, but visible to us as grandmothers, friends, mentors, spouses, and strangers. This intuition plays out in the variety of spiritual traditions, practices, and people that make up the communion of saints. Perhaps even more importantly for vast numbers of Catholics, this imagination encourages us to think about the events and encounters of daily life as the stuff of spirituality. Keeping to one's closet or retiring from the world are distinct and important aspects of spiritual practice, but only a few are called to be there permanently. Nor does withdrawal relieve one of the encounter with the burdens of everyday or difficult confreres. Rather, most men and women find themselves besieged with the labor of earning a living, raising children, negotiating life with a spouse, or dealing with difficult inlaws, illness, diminishment, and loss. That this might be the realm of encounter with the Divine is an audacious thought. Yet, the Catholic imagination leads us there. It is precisely in the midst of this that Christ came and continues to come. It is precisely in the midst of all this that discernment of spirits takes place. It is precisely in this that we are invited into the process of purgation so essential to the possibility of illumination and eventual union with God.

Finally, and all too suggestively, the Creed and the Catholic imagination embedded there give us a special sensitivity to paradox and to particularity. The Christian faith is founded on impossible paradoxes: Three in One, fully human, fully divine, life from death. These paradoxes are important. They can teach us a habit of what has been called by poet Rainer Maria Rilke, "living into the question." This does not mean the sort of critical questioning that demands an answer or solution, especially a quick one. Instead, these paradoxes can make us familiar with mystery, with wisdom that continually unfolds and reveals itself, with unexpected learning that has less to do with information than formation, with being shaped into people of generosity and compassion, mercy and faithfulness. We are invited to be people capable of living patiently into questions that have no easy answers, only more dimension and depth. This is what it means to walk in faith.

Paradox is a feature of the Catholic imagination, eloquently given voice in the Creed, as is a sensitivity to the particular. For all the vaulting theology contained in the Creed, all the abstract formulations about things ultimate, the Incarnation teaches us that specificity matters. God the Creator made a world that Scripture and Catholic teaching affirm is good and capable of mediating grace. Jesus took flesh, and that was essential to the divine plan. He was not a phantom, but fully human as well as fully divine—thus all that is human, all that is created is to be cherished in its specificity. Those particulars that have been overlooked are especially cherished in the Catholic imagination. The poor, the marginalized, the oppressed, the young, the unborn, the elderly, the ill, the vulnerable, the outcast, the immigrant, the displaced, the forgotten, the hidden, the widow, the orphan, the lonely, the despised: these have a special place in the Catholic view of things. They are part of our common life, a life divinely designed to flourish in justice, peace, and wholeness; a life revealed to us in the person of Jesus, who came to proclaim the kingdom or reign of God.

One last aspect of this attunement to particularity can yield a respect for variety and multiple expressions. While unity and a common life are dear to Catholics, it does not erase their deep respect for particularity. Saint and doctor of the Church, Francis de Sales, coined a word for it in the seventeenth century: *unidivers*, or "unity in diversity." The term implies neither rigid uniformity nor individualistic anarchy. Rather, it suggests our deep identity in love in the Mystical Body of Christ. The myriad customs, practices, prayer forms, movements, figures, initiatives, and teachings that can all claim to be part of Catholic spiritual traditions give credence to this claim.

These features of the Catholic imagination—communal, Trinitarian, sacramental, attunement to paradox and the particular—encoded in the Creed and carried by the tradition of the Church, are the essence of our story. Perhaps nineteenth century Jesuit Gerard Manley Hopkins' well-known "God's Grandeur" says it best and most aptly, in the language of poetry:

> The world is charged with the grandeur of God.
> It will flame out, like shining from shook foil;
> It gathers to a greatness, like the ooze of oil
> Crushed. Why do men then now not reck his rod?
> Generations have trod, have trod, have trod;
> And all is seared with trade; Bleared, smeared with toil;
> And wears man's smudge and shares man's smell:
> the soil
> Is bare now, nor can foot feel, being shod.
>
> And for all this, nature is never spent;
> There lives the dearest freshness deep down things;
> And though the last lights off the black West went
> Oh, morning, at the brown brink eastward, springs—
> Because the Holy Ghost over the bent
> World broods with warm breast and with ah!
> bright wings.

"GOD'S GRANDEUR"

Sources Cited

Catechism of the Catholic Church, http://www.usccb.org/catechism/text/.

Dogmatic Constitution on the Church (*Lumen Gentium*), Vatican Council II: The Basic Sixteen Documents, Copyright © 1996 by Reverend Austin Flannery, OP.

Elizondo, Virgil. *Guadalupe, Mother of the New Creation.* Maryknoll, NY: Orbis Books, 1997.

Hopkins, Gerard Manley. "God's Grandeur," 1877.

Kennedy, Michael. *Eyes on Jesus: A Guide for Contemplation.* New York: Crossroad, 1999.

New American Bible with Revised New Testament and Revised Psalms © 1991, 1986, 1970 Confraternity of Christian Doctrine, Washington, D.C.

Pope John XXIII: Essential Writings. Ed. Jean Maalouf. Modern Spiritual Masters Series. Maryknoll, NY: Orbis Books, 2008.

Romano Guardini: Spiritual Writings. Selected and translated by Robert A. Krieg. Maryknoll, NY: Orbis Books, 2005.

Saint Jerome. *Against Vigilantius.* Trans. Philip Schaff. Christian Catholics Ethereal Library, http://www.ccel.org.

Sor Juana Inés de la Cruz: Selected Writings. Trans. Pamela Kirk Rappaport. Classics of Western Spirituality Series. Mahwah, NJ: Paulist Press, 2005.

The Mary Page. The Marian Library/International Marian Research Institute. University of Dayton, http://campus.udayton.edu/mary/resources/engfive.html.

Further Reading: Classic and Contemporary

Cunningham, Lawrence. *A Brief History of Saints*. Oxford/Malden MA: Blackwell Publishing, 2005.

———. *Francis of Assisi: Performing the Gospel Life*. Grand Rapids, MI: William B. Eerdmans, 2004.

Day, Dorothy. *Loaves and Fishes*. Maryknoll, NY: Orbis Books, 1963.

Deberri, Edward, James Hug, Peter Henriot and Michael Schultheis. *Catholic Social Teaching: Our Best Kept Secret*. Maryknoll, NY: Orbis Books, 2003.

Downey, Michael. *Altogether Gift: a Trinitarian Spirituality*. Maryknoll, NY: Orbis Books, 2000.

Gutierrez, Gustavo. *We Drink from Our Own Wells*. Maryknoll, NY: Orbis Books, 1984.

Liturgy of the Hours

Mary in the Church: A Selection of Teaching Documents. Washington, DC: USCCB Publishing, 2003.

Pange Lingua

Woodward, Kenneth L. *Making Saints: How the Catholic Church Determines Who Becomes a Saint, Who Doesn't and Why*. Simon and Schuster, 1996.

Note: There are many translations of the classic texts in the Catholic spiritual tradition suggested below and throughout this handbook. Some noteworthy series of translations that can be recommended are the Paulist Press Classics of Western Spirituality series, which has many of the texts cited published under the author's name; the Institute of Carmelite Studies series on Carmelite authors; the Cistercian Publications translations of Cistercian Fathers; and the Modern Spiritual Masters series, published in the United States by Orbis Books.

Catherine of Siena, *The Dialogue*
John Eudes, *The Admirable Heart of Mary*
Guerric of Igny, *Liturgical Sermons*
Caryll Houselander, *The Reed of God*

SECTION FOUR

Walking the Way

Happy those whose way is blameless,
who walk by the teachings of the Lord.
Happy those who observe God's decrees,
who seek the Lord with all their heart.
They do no wrong;
they walk in God's ways.
You have given them the command
to keep your precepts with care.
May my ways be firm
in the observance of your laws!
Then I will not be ashamed
to ponder all your commands.
I will praise you with sincere heart
as I study your just edicts.
I will keep your laws;
do not leave me all alone.

PSALM 119:1–8

1. The Practice of the Catholic Spiritual Life

Before they were known as Christians, the early disciples of Jesus were known as followers of the Way. They traveled the path set forth for them by Jesus the Christ. The metaphor of the Way suggests that there is a journey aspect to this Catholic Christian life. If you have ever done more than stroll around the block or driven to the neighborhood grocery store, you will know that to embark on a journey—maybe a long road trip, an overseas excursion to a remote region, or a serious hike in the Rocky Mountains or along the Appalachian Trail—you need to have a guidebook, equipment, and advance preparation. You also need practices that will allow you to journey well. Carrying water, wearing sturdy shoes, and taking the right gear are essential for hikers. A passport, international funds, and knowledge of foreign customs are needed to go far abroad. But even more, you will need to become accustomed to the rigors of the mountains or the strenuous nature of traveling in remote geographies. The same is true for the Christian journey. The insights of the Church leaders gathered at the Second Vatican Council in the middle of the last century affirm this dynamic of the life of faith. Just as the entire body is a "pilgrim church," so all and each of us likewise are on a pilgrim's journey.

While the tradition assures us that we are each beloved daughters and sons of God, created in the divine image, we are also cautioned that we are still in the process of becoming fully what we were created to be. Each of us individually and all of us humans together do not reflect clearly the divine image in which we were created. That image, to use the language of tradition, is wounded, dimmed, or tarnished. We sin, we are spiritually and morally myopic or blind, we turn away, we fail to love, we are estranged from God, from each other, and from our deepest and truest selves. In our families, in our work places, our parishes, our larger faith communities, our neighborhoods, our countries, and in our world, we fail to live the Way. This is not to be gloomy or self-loathing. It is to be realistic. The kingdom Jesus preached is not fully present. While we do have the immense joy of seeing people and works in these varying milieus that evidence many are journeying toward the kingdom, we still experience God's promised reign of Love as both "already, but not yet." In a nutshell, we need to be formed into new people. The divine image needs to be healed, cleansed, or restored to make us into the people God created us to be so that we might contribute to the coming of the promised kingdom that Jesus proclaimed.

The word formation is the important word here. It is different from information, the buzz word of our present technological culture. Amassing a lot of data or putting together a portfolio of salutary ideas is good as far as it goes. But just having lots of information does not necessarily change us. In order to creatively and responsibly utilize information, we need to be people whose choices are focused by the kingdom perspective. We each need to be formed or shaped to more closely resemble the people God intends us to be. "We are the clay and you are the potter: we are all the work of your hands," says the prophet Isaiah (64:7). God's Spirit works creatively in our lives to encourage the process of formation.

Indeed, divine grace precedes and sustains all that we do. But we also must cooperate in the process by adopting practices and developing habits of mind and heart that predispose us to being formed into new persons.

Another way to look at it is to consider ourselves as disciples. Jesus gathered around himself a community of persons who responded to his message of the reign of God and who worked with him to invite all they met to be part of that kingdom. The word "disciple" is related to the word "discipline." One might perhaps think that discipline relates to punishment of some sort, of "being disciplined," or of following a rigid code of action. But a more apt definition of discipline is "training expected to produce a specific character or pattern of behavior, especially moral or mental improvement." If we are disciples, then we are in training, engaged in a program of readiness for the work of God's kingdom. Saint Paul's metaphor for the Christian life, the race, is appropriate here:

> *Therefore, since we are surrounded by so great a cloud of witnesses, let us rid ourselves of every burden and sin that clings to us and persevere in running the race that lies before us while keeping our eyes fixed on Jesus, the leader and perfecter of faith.*
>
> HEBREWS 12:1

We are being formed on the pattern of Christ. Again, we do not do this merely by ourselves. God is the initiator, the One who loves us so, who gives us life and longs for us to enjoy the fullness of life. But we must respond to that love. Many teachers in the Catholic spiritual traditions have taught that the desire to respond is inbuilt in us. Even though we are easily distracted, waylaid or misguided, buried deep within each of us is the longing for God. Part of being a disciple or being willing to be formed is the recovery or uncovering of that deep desire so that we can be clear about what is most essential in our lives. To do this we need to practice.

Father Ronald Rolheiser, a contemporary commentator on the Catholic spiritual life, offers a thought-provoking description of spirituality. He too has affirmed that the longing for God is inbuilt in human beings. Rolheiser describes a saint as someone who can channel this powerful desire or *eros* in a creative, life-giving, disciplined way. He goes on to give three fairly startling examples of people in the not-so-long-ago news who each experienced their deep desire in different ways; they either did or did not "do" something with it and they were either led to a full life or they flamed out, or some combination of the two. His first example is Mother Teresa of Calcutta, a "human dynamo" whose powerful desire was channeled toward God and the poor. Then Rohlhesier turns to rock star Janus Joplin, who died of an "overdose of life" at age twenty-seven. He describes her as not so different from Mother Teresa in that she too was a person with fiery *eros* and rare energy. But she was not able to focus herself and instead "went out in all directions and eventually created an excess and tiredness that led to a young death." Most of us, he explains, are a mix of the two. He chooses Princess Diana as such an example. She exhibited elements of both of the other women. Diana loved the the high life, spending millions on clothes and vacationing on yachts with rich boyfriends. However, she was also a person with tremendous compassion for the marginalized; she advocated for the victims of landmines and won the hearts of those she served. Rolheiser ends by saying that most of us are like Diana, engaged in a complex struggle of choice and commitment, drawn by desire but half the time not knowing how to fruitfully direct it. "Spirituality is about what we do with the fire inside us, about how we channel our *eros*. And how we do channel it, the disciplines and habits we choose to live by, will either lead to a greater integration or disintegration within our bodies, minds, and souls...in the way we are related to God, others, and the cosmic world" (*The Holy Longing*).

Catholics who are called to the religious life as a monk, nun, brother, or priest typically undergo a formal period of spiritual formation in order to embark on a disciplined pursuit of a fuller life. Generally this period early on involves a novitiate, a time when the entrant is seen as a novice or beginner, regardless of age or previous training. This is more than a period of orientation to the customs and expectations of the community. It is also a time of formal schooling, perhaps in theology or the history and practices of the particular order. Most importantly, the novitiate is a time of intentional formation in which the beginner is slowly unmade and remade. Prayer, spiritual conversation and direction, participation in the rhythms and work of the community or among those in need, and constant reflection about one's readiness to enter fully into the chosen life: these are some of the elements of training that a novice receives. Formation in religious life typically is overseen by a novice director, someone experienced in the specific expectations and spirit of the congregation.

For example, the Society of Jesus (the Jesuits) that sponsors so many schools inside and outside the United States expects the men wanting to join them to engage in a lengthy period of preparation. It may take up to ten years before a man is ordained a Jesuit priest. During that time, he is taken through a course of studies in philosophy, theology, and other humanities disciplines, and he is integrated into the work in which the Society is engaged. Most importantly, and central to Jesuit formation, is the initiate's participation in the Spiritual Exercises developed by Ignatius of Loyola, the order's founder. In his early formation, a young Jesuit takes part in an intensive thirty-day retreat, during which he meets daily with a spiritual director and spends his remaining hours praying with the series of meditations that make up the Exercises. The words of the Society's founder, Ignatius of Loyola, confirms the importance of the Exercises and periodic reflective retreat:

> By the term "Spiritual Exercises" we mean every method of examination of conscience, meditation, contemplation, vocal or mental prayer, and other spiritual activities....For, just as taking a walk, traveling on foot, and running are physical exercises, so is the name of spiritual exercises given to any means of preparing and disposing our soul to rid itself of all its

disordered affections and then, after their removal,
of seeking and finding God's will in the ordering of
our life for the salvation of our soul.

IGNATIUS OF LOYOLA: SPIRITUAL EXERCISES
AND SELECTED WORKS

These exercises aim toward the reorientation of all of the
entrant's capacities, his memory and understanding and will,
so that he may choose to align himself with the mission of
Christ in the world in whatever way God calls. Each year, a
Jesuit makes a shorter retreat to reaffirm his call, then after
many years, participates in the full thirty-day retreat once
again.

Lay people in the Church have not always had intentional
opportunities to immerse themselves in such a thorough and
formal reorientation of life. It is true that in the last decades,
opportunities to make retreats and experience spiritual guidance, including opportunities to make Ignatian retreats,
have increased. Many lay people are taking advantage of
this. Still, many do not or are not able to take advantage of
these offerings.

Despite this, a thoughtful, even profound reorientation
is still necessary for one to embark on the Way. This is why
spiritual practices are important for everyone, not just those
who choose religious life or the priesthood. They are possible
for and adaptable to people in all walks of life, genders, life
stages, and circumstances. However, one cannot learn something new or be genuinely formed without practice. Musicians
know this. Athletes know this. A basketball player or a vio-

linist may have natural talent, but will probably never really be a notable player unless he or she practices and hones the gift. So it is with the Christian life. The violinist must spend years doing scales before attempting a solo performance, the basketball player must practically live in the gym before making a shot that is "nothing but nylon" becomes second nature during competitive play. The Christian life is a Way that must be practiced.

Prompted by and sustained by God's grace, we can engage in any number of spiritual practices that move us closer to God in Christ. Among the most hallowed and recommended practices is prayer. But there are many others, beginning with the practice of the virtues. Each of these and the other varied practices highlighted here help to discipline us and to form us into the people God intends us to be.

2. Practice of the Virtues

It is common in American educational circles today to talk about "character education" or "teaching values." It is not always so clear what those values might be or what character traits are referred to in these discussions. In the traditions of Catholicism, it is clear what the spiritual values are. The chief human character traits are called the virtues, which are, simplistically defined, habits of thinking or willing that dispose one to act in ways that contribute to the good. Although the following do not exhaust the list of Catholic virtues, usually faith, hope, love, prudence (sound judgment), justice, temperance (restraint), and fortitude (courage) are named as the great virtues. In addition, for millennia the saints and spiritual teachers have spoken of the importance of other virtues such as humility, forgiveness, compassion, simplicity, courage, integrity, patience, and purity of heart. Virtues are habits that, in a foundational sense, are gifts of grace, but most of the great spiritual masters insist that the virtues can be practiced.

In the early Christian centuries, seekers went out into the deserts of Egypt, Syria, and Palestine to learn from the spiritual fathers and mothers who dwelt there. These ascetics were sought after. Their advice was often recorded in pithy little sayings or tales. The luminous virtues of the transformed life were etched on their faces, and they taught their disciples about the practice of the virtues:

> A brother asked an old man: What is humility? And the old man said: To do good to those who hurt you. The brother said: If you cannot go that far, what should you do? The old man replied: Get away from them and keep your mouth shut.

> Amma Theodora said: A teacher ought to be a stranger to love of domination, and a foreigner to vainglory, far from arrogance, neither deceived by flattery, nor blinded by gifts, nor a slave to the stomach, nor held back by anger, but rather should be patient, kind, and as far as possible humble. He ought to be self-disciplined, tolerant, diligent, and a lover of souls.

> DESERT WISDOM: SAYINGS FROM THE DESERT FATHERS

A habit is something that is strengthened by use and lost when neglected. Virtues, as habits, need the same sort of constant cultivation. Saint Francis de Sales, the seventeenth-century Savoyard bishop, wrote with great common sense about the practice of the virtues. His audience was lay women and men whose primary responsibilities were "in the world" with family and work, not within the cloister. He reminded them that most persons do not often have the occasion to practice heroic virtues, but do have frequent opportunity in daily life to practice what he called the "little virtues" such as patience, humility, temperance, integrity, and gentleness. Francis de Sales was certainly not suggesting that one put on a veneer of social pleasantness or that one endure abuse without murmuring, but rather that men and women genuinely practice the arts of relational charity, loving self and others as God has loved them. De Sales did not think that excessive exterior asceticism such as extreme penances, arduous fasts, or showy displays of piety were helpful. Rather, the cultivation of interior dispositions such as the little virtues, which he would say we had been shown by Jesus who is gentle and humble of heart (Matthew 11:29–30), was what was required to live the discipline of the Christian life.

Humility is one of the most cherished of spiritual virtues. Humility is not self-loathing or lack of self-esteem, but a balanced and clear-sighted knowledge, both of our gifts and of our weaknesses. It is a firm grasp of the fact that we are profoundly loved, forgiven, and called to the fullness of life, even as we stumble along, falling again and again. As a practice, de Sales says, humility shuns excessive pride or self-inflation.

More deeply, humility does not show itself off. But publicly effacing oneself is not the point. Being simple about one's gifts and one's weaknesses is the point. "Just as I would not parade knowledge even of what I actually know," Father de Sales says, "so, by contrast, I would not pretend to be ignorant of it. Humility conceals and covers the other virtues in order to preserve them, but it reveals them when charity so requires in order that we might enlarge, increase and perfect them" (*Introduction to the Devout Life*). Finally, humility invites us not only to know our own weaknesses, but, paradoxically, to love them, for they are the avenue through which we come to know our human vulnerability. As we then turn to our neighbor, our own true self-knowledge helps us to more clearly see others in our lives with more compassion. They too are gifted and weak, they too are loved as they stumble and fall. We are invited to be gentle toward them, as we are toward ourselves. Not self-deceptive or ignorant or indulgent about serious matters, unable to see where we fail and where we must grow and change, but gentle, like a loving parent who cheers on a child's attempts to walk by herself and offers a hand as she practices her first steps.

Forgiveness is another of the virtues that recent Christian commentators have seen fit to consider. The New Testament, especially the words and actions of Jesus himself, prompts these recent reflections. When Jesus taught his disciples to pray, a crucial element of what he taught was the art of forgiveness. The mantra is familiar to us all for we pray it often, "Give us this day our daily bread and forgive us our trespasses, as we forgive those who trespass against us." Moreover, at the most painful and desperate moment of his life, when he hung dying on the cross, Jesus modeled forgiveness for us. Speaking of those who were responsible for his impending death, he implored, "Father, forgive them for they know not what they do." What might this mean for us?

One of the most familiar of biblical parables is the story of the prodigal son found in the fifteenth chapter of the Gospel of Luke. It occurs in the context of Jesus' conversation with some religious men who are critical of the fact that he seemed to consort with people considered by the pious population to be sinners and thus unworthy. Jesus tells them the story of a man who had two sons, one who turned his back on the father and squandered his inheritance; the other who remained dutifully with the father (see Luke 15). The father rejoiced, as we know, when the unfaithful, irresponsible son returned. When the faithful son objected to the celebration at his brother's return, his father told him, "'But now we must celebrate and rejoice, because your brother was dead and has come to life again; he was lost and has been found'" (Luke 15:32).

The parable, first and foremost, demonstrates the mercy and forgiveness of the father, and by analogy, the mercy and forgiveness of God the Father. It is about a love so deep and wide that nothing can escape its embrace.

The parable is also a story about a child, a son in this case, who does not appreciate what he has, but who is lured by the glamour and seeming freedom beyond his father's home, and who then painfully sees what he has lost. This is analogously a story about each of us and our awakening to the mystery of a divine love that continues to seek us out, even when we turn away from it. But the story does not end there. It is also a tale about the other brother, the elder one, who is envious of his father's largess and complains about it loudly. This eldest is also each of us when we refuse to do what the father does, to love to the point of forgiveness, willing to have arms wide enough to welcome home the lost, the wayward, those who are cast out. At any given time in our lives, we may have insight into this story from one or another of these perspectives (or other perspectives of our own as well). But the parable is rich in implication. Forgiveness is central to God's identity. So, too, it must be to ours.

The pathos and beauty of the reunion between the penitent son and his compassionate father has inspired writers and authors over the years. The scene was arrestingly depicted by the seventeenth-century Dutch artist, Rembrandt, and it was an encounter with that masterful painting that led popular Catholic spiritual writer, Henri Nouwen, to reflect deeply on the theme of homecoming. In *The Return of the Prodigal Son*, the modern Dutch priest explored the meaning of the Parable of the Lost Son as it revealed the spiritual journey of his earlier countryman, the flamboyant painter who spent a profligate youth; as well as his own struggle with loneliness, jealousy, dejection, anger, and ultimate reconciliation and deeper encounter with God.

Nouwen's narrative suggests that forgiveness is not easy. Nor is it cheap. It leads us to remember that forgiveness does not bypass justice, pretending that wrong or sin or injury has not occurred. Nor does it circumvent the need for intervention or appropriate consequences if harm has been done or wrongs committed. But forgiveness is a practice that is central to Catholic faith. By our baptism, we are united with Christ and ushered into the divine mercy. We enter more deeply into the divine embrace each time we participate in the sacrament of reconciliation. Finally, each time we pray the Lord's Prayer, we pray for the grace to extend forgiveness just has God has forgiven us.

Although we have treated only two here in any detail, the virtues are many. But all the virtues are related to the greatest virtue of them all, love. The Scripture passage from Paul's first letter to the Corinthians, often chosen by couples for their wedding ceremonies, says it well. "Love is patient, love is kind. It is not jealous, [love] is not pompous, it is not inflated, it is not rude, it does not seek its own interests, it is not quick-tempered, it does not brood over injury, it does not rejoice over wrongdoing but rejoices with the truth. It bears all things, believes all things, hopes all things, endures all things" (13:4–7). This is clearly not a passage about love as romance, compatibility or sentimentality. It is about love as the creative, redemptive force that is stronger than death and more powerful than hell. In it we see that the practice of "little" virtues such as patience or humility or kindness are one with the great power of love which has God as its source and end. Doctor of the Church, Saint Francis de Sales, said it well when he wrote in his charming way, using homey analogies to make his point:

The king of bees never goes out into the fields without being surrounded by his little subjects. In like manner charity [love] never enters a heart without lodging both itself and its train of all the other virtues which it exercises and disciplines as a captain does his soldiers. It does not put them all to work all at once, nor at all times and in all places. The just man is 'like a tree planted near running water, that yields its fruit in due season,' for charity waters the soul and produces in it virtuous deeds, each in its proper time.

INTRODUCTION TO THE DEVOUT LIFE

Love is at the root of all virtues, but not every person will excel in every virtue. It is said of Blessed Damien of Molokai, the Belgian priest and member of the Congregation of the Sacred Hearts of Jesus and Mary, that he was a man of quick, even irascible temper who was perceived by many of his superiors as a troublemaker. When he was assigned to the colonial mission fields of Hawaii in the mid-nineteenth century, he became aware of a lepers' colony on one of the remote islands. Isolated, abandoned by family, government, and even the church ministries, these men, women, and children captured Damien's heart. He chose to live among them and serve them, eventually contracting the gruesome disease and dying of it. Damien is an example of a person who heroically practiced the virtues of compassion and solidarity. He never mastered his temper, nor did he master the art of getting along with his superiors. Nonetheless, he walked the Way. He practiced the virtues as he was able, some of them with an openheart-edness and vigor that has caused the Church to hold him up as one of those who embody Christ's holiness.

Saint Thérèse of Lisieux is another example of a person who consciously cultivated the virtues. Thérèse, known to posterity as the "Little Flower," was a rather ordinary girl from a late nineteenth-century middle class French family. As a youngster, she was petulant and overly sensitive, but as she describes it, God changed her heart and she began to see her life as it was bathed in God's love. She eventually was drawn to the enclosed Carmelite convent in Lisieux. Although she had a great passion to live heroically—she adored Joan of Arc and other martyrs and dreamed of being sent to the mission fields—she knew herself to be young, weak, and imperfect, a "little bird" without strength and wings. Yet she came to believe that, despite her insignificance, she could live love by treating others with love. Jesus would be the eagle bearing her on his wings. She set about to deal gently and lovingly with all the members of the Carmel community, despite the fact that some were difficult and abrasive women. Her way of practicing virtue was to do little things with great love. Thérèse's "little way," sometimes called the way of "spiritual childhood," led her to believe:

> To be little is not attributing to oneself the virtues that one practices, believing oneself capable of any-thing, but to recognize that God places this treasure in the hands of His little child to be used when neces-sary; but it remains always God's treasure. Finally, it

is not to become discouraged over one's little faults, for children fall often, but they are too little to hurt themselves very much.

ST. THÉRÈSE OF LISIEUX: *ESSENTIAL WRITINGS*

The virtues are many; not all will excel in every virtue. But all the virtues are habits of heart and mind that can be practiced as we walk the Way. Indeed, the practicing is the Way.

Here there is not Greek and Jew, circumcision and uncircumcision, barbarian, Scythian, slave, free; but Christ is all and in all.

Put on then, as God's chosen ones, holy and beloved, heartfelt compassion, kindness, humility, gentleness, and patience, bearing with one another and forgiving one another, if one has a grievance against another; as the Lord has forgiven you, so must you also do. And over all these put on love, that is, the bond of perfection. And let the peace of Christ control your hearts, the peace into which you were also called in one body. And be thankful. Let the word of Christ dwell in you richly, as in all wisdom you teach and admonish one another, singing psalms, hymns, and spiritual songs with gratitude in your hearts to God. And whatever you do, in word or in deed, do everything in the name of the Lord Jesus, giving thanks to God the Father through him.

COLOSSIANS 3:11–17

3. Practices of Prayer

Often when the term "spirituality" is brought up, prayer is what immediately comes to mind. This is, of course, a natural association. Several centuries ago, the associated term, spiritual life, was used in Catholic circles precisely to refer only to prayer and the inner life. It is still common for people to assume this. But spirituality as it is understood today (and actually as it has always been practiced) is not merely about the interior life, but about a life transformed by God's Spirit. Our lives are both inner and outer, personal and communal, private and public. Still, the interior is absolutely essential, and any consideration of transformation must assign an important role to prayer.

We have already suggested that the Catholic spiritual life is rooted in the shared experience of liturgical prayer, and that praying with the rest of the Church at the eucharistic liturgy, at the Liturgy of the Hours, and at other services deeply shapes us. We are immersed in the common language of the Scriptures, the unfolding cycles of the liturgical year and the sanctified rhythms of the day. Yet we need as well to establish other personalized ways of communicating with God and with one another in the communion of saints. We need to learn ways to pray that carry the deep longing at the core of our being to its source, God. We need to learn some of the arts of self-awareness, reflection, and attentiveness to the movements of our hearts in order to pray and live from that inner core.

In a fascinating recent book, *Tree of Life*, scholar Steven

Chase used the metaphor of a tree to describe the rich variety of prayer forms that have developed over the centuries. He first describes prayer as a way of life, a habitat in which to dwell. This is an important insight. While it is legitimate to say that one can "go to prayer" or "say one's prayers," it is even more important, and more traditional, to think of prayer as involving the stuff of life: "a way of being, feeling, sensing, understanding, doing, dwelling, caring, seeing, knowing, imagining, reasoning, falling, failing, suffering, relating, and transforming." As Chase insists, to know prayer, one must pray.

VOCAL PRAYER

The traditional way to begin any discussion of personal Catholic prayer is to begin with the treasury of vocal prayers that belong to the tradition. A vocal prayer is a prayer that is spoken aloud or voiced. First among the many that we voice, of course, is the Lord's Prayer, the common prayer that Jesus taught. This prayer not only defines us as Christians, it is a rich resource for continued reflection; indeed it has been for centuries. Saint Thomas Aquinas, father of the church, declared it to contain "all that we ought to desire and all that we ought to avoid" (*Catechetical Instructions*). Other familiar vocal prayers are the Hail Mary, the Glory Be, the Salve Regina (Hail Holy Queen), the Memorare (Remember O Most Blessed Virgin Mary), and Angel of God. Then there are litanies that we may pray as individuals or at our common worship. They include, among many others, the Divine Praises ("Blessed be God, blessed be His Holy Name...."), the Litany of the Sacred

Heart ("Heart of Jesus, Son of the Eternal Father, have mercy on us; Heart of Jesus, formed in the womb of the Virgin Mother by the Holy Ghost, have mercy on us…"), and the Marian Litany of Loreto ("Holy Mother of God, pray for us; Most honored of Virgins, pray for us…"). With its repetitive rhythm and responsive pattern, a litany draws us into the mystery and the presence of the persons we invoke, connecting our personal intentions to the intentions of all those who pray or have prayed these hallowed words. Sometimes vocal prayer can be trivialized and perceived either as empty ritual or as a sort of duty that one must perform. Nothing could be farther from the true meaning of these ancient forms of address. If prayed with the heart, as well as the lips, vocal prayers can give our deepest longings and reverence form. They can also usher us into the divine presence, laying before us the rich insights of centuries and helping us to begin to speak of the God who, in the end, is beyond all names.

Vocal prayer is generally spoken, but it may also be sung. Indeed, words set to music may enable us to express what mere words themselves cannot capture. The many seasons of our lives and the sorrows and joys we carry in our hearts can all be borne by a thousand different melodies. Perhaps we can appreciate this truth when we think of the many Christmas carols that evoke deep feelings of comfort and wonder. In fact, many of the texts of traditional carols that we sing at the feast of the Incarnation, the Nativity of Christ, are treasures of theological depth and richness, worth reflecting upon during the season instead of being relegated to background music in the shopping mall. One of the most ancient of these hymns,

Corde natus ex parentis ("Of the Father's Love Begotten"), was composed in the fifth century by Prudentius, a layman and governmental official of the Roman Empire, one of the greatest Latin Christian poets.

Perhaps we might also recall a song sung at the funeral of a loved one and the extent to which that song continues to live in us, or reflect on the extent to which our knowledge of the Psalms is inextricably tied to the chant tones or melodies that carry them in the liturgy. Certainly at our common liturgies, the use of sung prayer is important. But we may also use song as prayer in small groups or alone.

Vocal prayer is not always formulaic, however, and we may find ourselves spontaneously praying aloud, calling upon the names of Jesus or Mary, expressing gratitude, or asking for strength and aid. Or we may simply delight in the goodness of our God, sharing our thoughts and dreams with Jesus as companion and friend. Or we may pray aloud within the context of a faith-sharing community or prayer group by interceding for another person, asking that they be healed, protected, or graced in one way or another. Intercession is, of course, one of the most practiced forms of prayer. We all find ourselves asking for healing or aid or graces for those we love or for those whose suffering moves us. Intercessory prayer is grounded in the Catholic sensibility of the communion of saints and our shared life in the Mystical Body. We experience ourselves, not as separate entities adrift in an impersonal universe, but as persons connected to one another through the mystery of a God who is both personal and intimate. When we intercede for one another, as when we ask for ourselves, we are entrusting ourselves to the mercy and the generosity of our good God.

It is helpful to remember that prayer is not a mechanical process. It certainly is not magic. It is not simply a matter of wishing or desiring something very hard and then having that wish granted. God "answers" prayer sometimes in ways we cannot anticipate. Intercessory prayer places us and the ones for whom we pray in the divine presence, and we must often leave it at that. However, we should also recall that prayer does not absolve us from acting when it is possible. For example, if we pray for relief for the poor, we should assess our own ability to help alleviate poverty. If we are moved by the loneliness of the elderly, we might want to consider participating in a parish project of visiting the homebound or nursing care facilities. If we pray for an end to hunger, we might contribute to Catholic Charities or another humanitarian organization or make donations to a local food bank. Perhaps our intercessory prayer might be "answered" by our being inspired to see ways we can participate in the good that God is doing in the world.

When we pray, we voice our deepest longings. This in itself changes us and those around us. Praise, thanksgiving, intercession, adoration, petition, consecration, and dedication: all these stances that we take in relationship to the divine, all these modalities of prayer, may be voiced aloud.

MENTAL PRAYER

Not all prayer, of course, is voiced. The tradition offers us many examples of prayers that involve the internalized use of the mind in various ways. Certainly, familiar prayers may be silently repeated. But beyond that, there are many wise ways to go to God in prayer using our mental capacities. Particularly, we might point to three fruitful forms of mental prayer: *lectio divina*, imaginative meditation, and the daily *Examen*. *Lectio* has for centuries been associated with monastic devotion, but today is widely practiced by all sorts of people: monks, lay, and religious alike. *Lectio divina* (the term means "sacred reading") is a way of praying with Scripture that involves a flexible four-fold movement and allows the Word of God to be deeply internalized and personalized.

Lectio Divina

Monks have long described their approach to the Bible as "eating the bread of the Word." In a sense, *lectio* mirrors the act of eating. A bit of food is broken off, taken in, savored, enjoyed, chewed so that it may be ingested, and then becomes the nutrient that sustains and allows life to flourish. In *lectio*, a small segment of Scripture is read for literal content, then considered and turned over in the mind. A word, phrase, or insight may stand out and become the focal point; it may be repeated, savored, worried, prayed. One may address God directly, holding a loving conversation about the taste and texture of that nourishing word; then one may simply rest with what has taken place, what one has tasted and seen.

This is a very different practice than studying the Bible for its theological or historical insights (very good in itself, but not always the only way to pray). It is certainly different from using the Bible as a proof text to prove a point or from letting the Bible fall open to a page for inspiration. *Lectio* allows the good Word to be genuinely integrated into one's daily life; it allows the Scripture to become the language of one's own heart. You are what you eat.

Imaginative Meditation

Another approach to the integration of Scripture is to engage in imaginative meditation. Especially associated with the Ignatian tradition, this sort of prayer involves the use of all the senses to enter into and engage with the scriptural narrative.

Here is a small example: Place yourself in a scene described in Scripture, say, the story in Luke 10 which describes Jesus' visit to the house of Mary and Martha in Bethany. Often this text is referred to as the Martha and Mary story. Imagine the scene, the people, the sights, sounds, and smells. You might imagine yourself as one or more of those figures. Perhaps you are Martha, busily preparing the meal, anxious about being a hostess; perhaps you are a bystander watching from afar as Jesus comes to visit. Perhaps you are Mary, awed by her Lord's visit, longing to sit at his feet and listen to him speak. Perhaps you see the decoration in the room, hear the voices of the townsfolk outside, smell the dinner being prepared. Perhaps you are a character who is not described in the passage. Ask yourself how you feel, what you might say, and how the action might develop as the story unfolds. You do not need to keep to the text, but experience the scene as if you were truly present and let it unfold as it will. Praying with Scripture this way doesn't necessarily require one to seek a theological insight, but a personal one. You may gain insight into your relationship with God, or you may be inspired or challenged by what occurs during your meditation, carrying from it images and questions that will help you grow.

A variant of this very vivid and involved sort of prayer was long popular, well before Ignatius of Loyola used it so creatively in his Exercises. For centuries, Catholics meditated on the Passion of Christ, sometimes by entering into the dramatic scene in the personalized way just described, sometimes by using prayer books that directed their thoughts. Looking to the wound in Christ's side, one could meditate on the mystery of love poured out there. Seeing him crowned with thorns, one might feel great compassion. The Lenten practice of making the Stations of the Cross and empathetically entering into the mystery of divine condescendence by meditatively following the events leading up to the crucifixion is an outgrowth of the meditation on the Passion.

A dramatic episode in the spiritual life of late thirteenth century Franciscan tertiary, Angela of Foligno, illustrates the manner in which such meditation on the passion has played out in the tradition, and the way in which personal appropriation of insight might be gained through the meditative process:

On Wednesday of Holy Week, I was meditating on the death of the Son of God incarnate, and trying to empty my soul of everything else so I could be more recollected in his passion and death. I had only one care, only one desire, and that was to find the best way to empty my soul from everything else in order to have a more vivid memory of the passion and death of the Son of God.

Suddenly, while I was engrossed in this effort and desire, a divine word sounded in my soul: "My love for you has not been a hoax." These words struck me a mortal blow. For immediately the eyes of my soul were opened and I saw that what he had said was true. I saw his acts of love, everything that the Son of God had done, all that he had endured in life and death—this suffering God-man—because of his inexpressible and visceral love. Seeing in him all the deeds of true love, I understood the perfect truth of what he had said, that "his love for me had not been a hoax," but that he had loved me with a most perfect and visceral love. I saw on the other hand, the exact opposite in myself, because my love for him had never been anything but playing games, never true. Being aware of this was a mortal blow and caused such intolerable pain that I thought I would die.

THE BOOK OF BLESSED ANGELA OF FOLIGNO

Examen

The scriptural mysteries are a boundless source of life from which we can draw, and *lectio* or imaginative meditation can make the Word come alive in very personalized ways. But Scripture is not the sole text from which we can read the story of God-with-us. Our own daily experience can also be a text upon which we can see the imprint of God's gracious hand. The *Examen* is a form of mental prayer that helps one to pay attention to the way in which God is present in one's life. The Examen originally was thought of as an examination of conscience, a formal method of reflecting at the end of the day about where one had failed to live according to the dictates of God. More recently, the *Examen* has been developed as an examination of consciousness, a method of looking back upon one's day and replaying it, to discern the indentations of the divine footprints. One may have missed the fact that God was present in the interactions with a co-worker or child, or that in the rush of daily duties grace abounded. Placing oneself and one's every action in God's presence, giving thanks, asking for forgiveness, making resolutions, accepting gifts: this daily practice sensitizes one to the way God weaves into the fabric of our lives.

In their contemporary rendering of the *Examen* entitled *Sleeping With Bread*, Dennis and Matthew Linn and Sheila Fabricant Linn explore and make accessible to ordinary people the many facets of this ancient practice. They simplify the *Examen* to its essentials:

For many years we have ended each day the same way.
We light a candle, becoming aware of God's loving
presence, and take about five minutes of quiet while
we ask ourselves two questions.
For what moment today am I most grateful?
For what moment today am I least grateful?

SLEEPING WITH BREAD

This simple prayer practice becomes the vehicle through
which God's activity in the ordinary fabric of everyday life
and our response to that presence becomes conscious.

Some people enjoy a less formal but nonetheless equally
intentional approach to attending to the Divine in their lives.
The Practice of the Presence of God is the title of a little book
that since the late seventeenth century has guided Catholics.
Written by a humble French Carmelite brother who spent his
adult life working in the monastery kitchen, Brother Lawrence
of the Resurrection taught a familiar, constant attentiveness
to God in the midst of everyday activity. The practice of the
presence of God, he said, "...is to take delight in and become
accustomed to his divine company." He encourages the practice of praising God throughout the day, pausing the daily
acitivities, "even during our reading and writing, no matter
how spiritual" to praise God and give thanks.

A related practice that hails from the same period but
which has retained its currency over the centuries is described
in the work attributed to Jean-Pierre de Caussade, *Abandonment to Divine Providence*. This spiritual guide's focus is upon
what he calls the "sacrament of the present moment." Central

to this easily adaptable practice is the knowledge that God is ever-present, sustaining and caring for us, even in the most routine and tedious of occupations or responsibilities. De Caussade urges his readers to embrace the present as an opportunity to peer with the eyes of faith into what is often an opaque experience. For "every moment is crammed with infinite riches....There is never a moment when God does not come forward in the guise of some suffering or some duty, and all that takes place within us, around us and through us both includes and hides his activity." The focus in this practice is upon finding God in whatever is given to one, not in the sense that God "plans" or "orchestrates" every event of life. (Normative Catholic teaching affirms that humans have free will and that God, while extending grace, allows human choices which have their own consequences.) Even in the most murky of situations, divine grace can be discovered.

This last piece of wisdom is one that is applicable well beyond the spiritual discipline of "abandonment" recommended by Pierre de Caussade. For most of us, it is all too easy to assume that God is present and active in our lives when things are going well, especially if we have had a fairly comfortable life and have been challenged only by the ordinary circumstances of being human. But sometimes our lives unravel, tragedy takes hold, we are unmoored, and God seems to have disappeared. How, in such circumstances, might we reconcile our experience with our belief in an all-powerful, all-knowing God? More will follow about spiritual "dark nights," but suffice it to say that the tradition invites us into an encounter with the divine presence no matter what life hands us. God does not "cause" suffering or "ordain" that the young die or the innocent suffer. Our faith is in a love that is stronger than death. Our belief is in a new life that rises out of the crucible of pain and suffering. Our hope is in a God who meets us and accompanies us in every moment, light or dark, joy-filled or sorrowful, abundant or lacking. The point is that prayer is the pathway into the discovery of such a God. As strange, difficult, and even anguished as it may seem, our prayer must be wide and deep and adventurous enough to hold together these paradoxes, to let God be God, to move into mystery, to not always seek answers, but wait patiently to be shown.

Richard Hauser, a contemporary Jesuit spiritual writer, wrestles with the question of suffering and faith. He concludes:

> Where is our God in our suffering? We Christians do not have a fully satisfying explanation for why the world contains so much suffering. But we have something better: we have the power to deal with the suffering. We know where our God is during suffering. Our God is with us... with us in all the senseless accidents and ruptured relationships and interior brokenness of our lives. And we cannot claim to be living a fully Christian life until we believe and live this dimension of the Gospel, until we trust God's presence and power working through our own "thorns in the flesh," Gethsemanes and Calvarys.
>
> *FINDING GOD IN TROUBLED TIMES*

CONTEMPLATIVE PRAYER

Prayer may be vocal or mental, practiced on one's knees or while making supper. It may involve music, take the form of a simple conversation, or be an openness to discovering grace in each moment. Prayer may also be an entry into an awareness that goes beyond words. "Contemplative prayer" and "contemplation" are terms used in a variety of ways. They may sometimes refer to an advanced form of interiority described by some of the great mystics of the tradition like Teresa of Ávila and John of the Cross, an interiority which implies a radical union with the Divine, a state in which God is said to act directly in and through the mystic. But more commonly, contemplative prayer refers to practices that emphasize silence and receptivity as the primary modalities of relating to God. Many of the great early Church fathers like Augustine, Gregory the Great, or Bernard of Clairvaux understood contemplation as a way of perceiving the world: a simplified, whole-seeing that gives birth to faith, hope, and love.

Contemplative prayer tends to wordlessness and the unification of thought, feeling, and desire so that the energies of the whole person are gathered into focus. It calms, rather than activates, the various faculties that are generally used in other sorts of prayer. In contemplation, one allows oneself to be acted upon, rather than acting as an agent. One becomes radically open to the Spirit's prompting. To approach it from another vantage point, contemplative prayer has to do with allowing oneself to be formed by and into an image that challenges the present images with which one lives.

Centering prayer is today one of the most widely taught forms of contemplative practice. The Cistercian Order has been active in teaching and disseminating information on centering prayer through its Contemplative Outreach Programs. It was drawn from ancient prayer practices of the Christian contemplative heritage, especially the fourteenth century anonymous work, The Cloud of Unknowing, and distilled into a simple method of prayer in the 1970s by three Trappist (Cistercians of the Strict Observance) monks, Father William Meninger, Father Basil Pennington, and Abbot Thomas Keating. Centering prayer typically involves a twice-a-day, twenty-minute period, during which the devotee sits quietly, but does not dwell on particular thoughts, images, or formulaic devotions. Instead, a single repeated word or simple phrase, chosen for its personal meaning and as a symbol of one's consent to God's action within, is offered in love. If thoughts come, they are to be relinquished with a return to the sacred Word. The fruits of centering prayer are not discernable during the practice itself, but only gradually in the fabric and texture of one's life.

In his New Seeds of Contemplation, twentieth-century monk Thomas Merton wrote rhapsodically of contemplation as:

> Contemplation is life itself, fully awake, fully active, fully aware that it is alive. It is spiritual wonder. It is spontaneous awe at the sacredness of life, of being. It is gratitude for life, for awareness, and for being. It is a vivid realization of the fact that life and being in

us proceed from an invisible, transcendent, and infinitely abundant Source. Contemplation is, above all,
awareness of the reality of that Source. It knows the
Source, obscurely, inexplicably, but with a certitude
that goes beyond reason and beyond simple faith...
It is a more profound depth of faith, a knowledge
too deep to be grasped in images, in words, or even
in clear concepts.

NEW SEEDS OF CONTEMPLATION

MYSTICISM

In discussions of contemplative prayer, the topic of mysticism
often comes up. Perhaps it might be useful to begin with a
consideration of what mysticism is and is not. To begin with,
the term itself, like the term spirituality, is used in a variety of
often conflicting ways. Not infrequently, people will refer to
moments of intense insight—the sight of a beautiful vista, a
deep personal encounter, a transcendent religious moment—
as mystical. The veils that have shrouded their perceptions
of things seem to have been lifted. Equally frequent is the
equation of the term "mystical" with what might be described
as paranormal phenomenon. Visions of varying kinds, locu-
tions (hearing voices), levitation, raptures, ecstasies, stigmata,
premonitions, strange occurrences, and so forth all tend to be
described in common parlance as "mystical." This is not at all
what the Catholic tradition would describe as mysticism.

The root of the word itself is related to the concept of
mystery and also to the mysteries of the Catholic faith. It is

not that these mysteries of faith are occult or confusing, but that they reach into a dimension of reality that cannot be fully explained or grasped by human means. Mysticism then may be viewed as an immediate, direct, intuitive knowledge of God and of ultimate things attained through personal religious experience. Noted scholar Bernard McGinn cautions us that the accounts of mystics are not directly accessible to us, that all we have is reports and accounts of experiences that are difficult to describe. We have no access to another person's experience. We are therefore, as readers, receiving a mediated experience. We are encountering statements about experience, albeit in the form of first person narratives or autobiographical accounts of special unitive or visionary experiences of God. He also cautions us that we should not consider accounts of mystical experience as free floating outside of tradition. Instead, the Christian mysticism tradition is embedded in the activities of reading, interpreting, and praying the Bible and other classic texts.

McGinn explains the term mysticism "as a part of or element of religion...a process or way of life...an attempt to express a direct consciousness of the presence of God." Returning to our own modern interest in the topic, it might be noted that the authenticity of any "mystical experience," however, is not dependent on the form of that experience, but solely on the quality of life that follows. The mystical life—and the term "life" is important here—is characterized by enhanced vitality, productivity, serenity, and joy as the inner and outward aspects harmonize in union with God. Usually a one-time experience, a spiritual "high" does not qualify a person as a mystic. Rather, someone may be known as a mystic if he or she habitually dwells in the divine presence (although that presence in itself may not always be felt) and exhibits some of the salutary fruits of relationship with the Divine.

The heightened experiences that may happen to all of us—the mountain top ecstasies—are perhaps an ordinary sort of mysticism in the sense that we are made aware of the mystery at the heart of our lives; we are given perspective. We may even be given insight into God's goodness or mercy or justice. But in terms of paranormal experiences, these are not in themselves mysticism. Paranormal events can be part of prayer, or they may have nothing at all to do with God. They may be caused by normal or abnormal physiological processes or conjured up by an undisciplined mind. The great Carmelite teachers of prayer and countless others in the tradition affirm that unusual experiences in prayer are generally secondary phenomena occasioned by the purgative process, which sometimes destabilizes a person physically and psychically. In some cases, these paranormal events may be part of an encounter with the Divine, but in themselves, they are not mystical. It is the union of wills, the cleaving of lives, and the aligning of hearts that is at the core of the mystical. The Way is a journey, a path, a process, not a series of heightened experiences to be collected or achieved. It is about God's love and longing for each of us and about the longing that we have to return that love and share it with others.

VISUAL IMAGERY AND IMAGELESS PRAYER

Many traditional accounts that might be deemed mystical speak of moving into a realm beyond present concepts and images. Similarly, centering prayer and other types of contemplative prayer eschew the use of images. These, however, are not necessarily "higher" forms of prayer. Rather, contemplative prayer should be viewed as a practice to which some persons are genuinely drawn and to which others may not be. It is true, however, that as we mature in faith, hope, and love and in the wisdom of the spiritual life, our prayer often becomes more simplified. Perhaps it might be helpful to think of our relationship with God as a long loving marriage: at some point, couples who have experienced a lifetime together no longer need to use a great many words, but may simply enjoy being in one another's presence. As we grow in faith, we may seem to employ fewer words, have less need to have all our burning questions answered, or have less complicated ideas and focused images of God. A simple metaphor or a loving word may do, a gentle surrender into unknowing, an abandonment of all else but gratitude, or an embrace of the constant, restless longing.

Nevertheless, we are each unique, and to pray well does not mean that we must pray a certain way. Some individuals find the use of visual images in prayer suits them well. The practices of imaginative meditation mentioned above utilize visual images internally. But the use of external imagery is a very rich part of the Catholic tradition as well. The innumerable images depicted in statuary, paintings, tapestries, woodcarving, and stained glass windows that decorate Catholic churches all over the world testify to the importance of the visual in the Catholic imagination. They testify to the sacramental sense that God works through the created order and that the invisible is made manifest to us through the visible.

Praying with the sacred imagery that surrounds us is more than just a pedagogical exercise. The visual depiction of the mysteries of faith, for example, the annunciation (the angel Gabriel's announcement to Mary that she is to bear a child) or the presentation (Jesus' parents present their firstborn in the Temple), not only recount the stories of the Bible and tell us what happened, they are available for our reflection and meditative consideration as well. They convey the greater inexpressible fact that God took human flesh. More personally, they may speak to us the truth that we too are asked to utter our fiat: "Let it be done to me according to your will." Like Mary and Joseph, we bring our most cherished gifts to the altar as an offering to God.

The formal practices of using visual imagery in prayer are important to recognize. One example is the icon-gazing, so characteristic of the Eastern Orthodox churches. The practice has moved beyond its orthodox context and garnered enthusiasm in Catholic circles in recent years. An icon is not simply an illustration, but a sacred "window" on the heavenly realm. The painting style is intentionally two-dimensional, having only width and a height. Depth, the third (physical) dimension, seems to be absent. But the third dimension of an icon goes beyond what the eye can see, as it is spiritual.

These sacred windows depicting Jesus Christ, the Mother of God, or an angel or a saint enable someone who is praying to gaze into the heavenly realm. In turn, the heavenly presence gazes upon those who pray.

The late Henri Nouwen, modern spiritual writer and priest, has written insightfully about the use of icons, a practice which he explored for several years. The fruits of his loving gaze upon several classic Eastern Orthodox icons is recorded in *Behold the Beauty of the Lord*:

> I have never seen the house of love more beauti-
> fully expressed than in the icon of the Holy Trinity,
> painted by Andrew Rublev in 1425 in memory of the
> great Russian saint Sergius (1313-1392). For me the
> contemplation of this icon has increasingly become
> a way to enter more deeply in the mystery of divine
> life while remaining fully engaged in the struggles
> of our hate-and-fear-filled world.
>
> *BEHOLD THE BEAUTY OF THE LORD*

An icon is not merely a work of art that illustrates the Scriptures. It constitutes a confession of religious truths that, when "read" prayerfully over years, become internalized wisdom.

There are also classic visual images that come to us directly from our western Catholic tradition, too. An example is the Sacred Heart, which during the modern era and until the mid-twentieth century was, along with the image of the Virgin Mary as the Immaculate Conception, the defining image of global Catholicism. The Sacred Heart in the form familiar to most Catholics—Jesus pointing to the thorn-circled heart exposed on his breast—is visible across the Catholic landscape today in statuary, stained glass windows, holy cards, and devotional paintings. But this familiar image was developed over a long period of time through the cumulative prayer and theological reflection of the Church and its people.

The scriptural roots of the image go back to the allegorical reflections of Church fathers like Origen, Augustine, Ambrose, Cyprian, and Jerome. They developed several central ideas that would undergird the developing devotion by reading Scripture. Typical of the reflections is Saint Ambrose's lyric hymn:

> Drink of Christ, for he is the rock
> from which the water springs.
> Drink of Christ, for he is the fountain of life.
> Drink of Christ, for he is the stream whose torrent
> brought joy to the city of God.
> Drink of Christ for he is peace.
> Drink of Christ for streams of living water flow
> from his body.

> "EXPLANATION OF THE PSALMS"
> QUOTED IN *SACRED HEART: GATEWAY TO GOD*

The image readily calls to mind the nineteenth chapter of the Gospel of John, which tells of the blood and water flowing from the pierced side of Christ at his death. Allegories such as this one speak of the Church, the Body of Christ, as born from this pierced side. Christ was the fountain of life. His wounded side was the fountain from which springs of living water—the sacraments—flowed. The blood of the Eucharist and the waters of baptism were the waters from which all might drink and receive eternal life. Echoing the psalms, Christ was also the rock from which that water sprang. Saint Ambrose of Milan would compose this lyric hymn in the fifth century.

The fathers enriched the allegory with imagery from the Song of Songs. They saw the Church, like Eve, as born from the side of Christ, and the church-bride as the issue of the bridegroom's heart. Further, they read the narrative of the Last Supper and interpreted the beloved disciple who rested on the breast of Jesus as John. For them, John was a contemplative, one who rested near the heart of God and became intimate with the wisdom discovered there. These early fathers located the site of the human-divine intimacy in the pierced body of the Savior, from whom grace flowed and who offered refuge and wisdom to a beloved disciple in prayer.

As Christianity matured into the middle ages, these early ideas were expanded. Allegory gave way to an intensely personal piety focused on the wounds of the Body. Visual depictions of the wounds began to appear as devotional objects, sometimes seen in concert with the implements of the passion, but often by themselves. The side would especially become the focus of private devotion. It became the symbol par excellence of the loving relationship between Creator and creatures. It was the portal through which salvation was gained, the aperture through which new life was gestated in the womb of God and was birthed. Thus an anonymous Carthusian of the fourteenth century might have composed this beautiful prayer:

> Enter, O my soul, enter into the right side of thy crucified Lord. Enter through this blessed wound into the centre of the all-loving Heart of Jesus, pierced through for love of thee. Take thy rest in the clefts of the Rock sheltered from the tempests of the world. Enter into thy God! Covered with herbage and fragrant flowers, the path of life lies open before thee. This is the way of salvation, the bridge leading to heaven.
>
> *ANCIENT DEVOTIONS TO THE SACRED HEART OF JESUS*
> *BY CARTHUSIAN MONKS OF THE XIV-XV CENTURIES*
> QUOTED IN *SACRED HEART: GATEWAY TO GOD*

In the high middle ages, visionary and mystic experiences of the divine heart abounded. The contemplative who desired union would drink from the opened side, seek intimacy in the refuge of the wound, and be incorporated into God though that bleeding portal. In addition, the side of Christ with its flowing streams came to be seen in a heightened eucharistic light. Thirteenth century women in the circle of the Rhineland monastery of Helfta-like Gertrude the Great and Mechtilde of Hackborn, were recording visions of Christ that appeared to them revealing his heart. It is at this time that the mystical motif of the "exchange of hearts" between Christ and a devotee emerged. This experience was variously described by medieval holy women Catherine of Siena, Catherine de Ricci, and Lutgard of Awyiere. During the fifteenth century, the devotion spread beyond cloistered walls into the emergent tradition of lay piety. It showed itself in multitudes of prayers, poems, and artistic expressions. But it was still not the form of the image we recognize today. The Sacred Heart was generally depicted as hanging from the cross, as a freestanding image, or as discovered alongside the implements of the passion.

In the sixteenth century, the devotion spread to the young Jesuit Order and found a new expression in the Salesian spiritual tradition founded by Francis de Sales and Jane de Chantal. The community of the Visitation of Holy Mary that these two saints co-founded was deeply imbued with the diffuse verbal and visual imagery associated with the heart. Salesian spirituality saw the world as a world of hearts: the heart of God which created human hearts in its own image and likeness, linked by the crucified heart of Christ. The tradition focused on the inner transformation of ordinary Christians. Jesus was to live in each human heart through the practice of the virtues. These virtues were realized as they were lived between people, heart to heart.

The early Sisters of the Visitation considered themselves imitators of the virtues of the Sacred Heart or daughters of the Sacred Heart of Jesus. But it was not until later in the seventeenth century that a member of the Visitation Order in the monastery of Paray le Monial, Margaret Mary Alacoque, had a series of "great revelations" about the Sacred Heart. Those revelations were made known by her Jesuit confessor, Claude de la Colombiere, and promoted by other Jesuit confreres, and the devotion as we are familiar with it today emerged. The liturgical feast of the Sacred Heart, observed today on the Friday after the feast of Corpus Christi (the Body and Blood of Christ), celebrates the mystery of the Eucharist, first Friday observance, and the themes of adoration and reparation. All these stem from the visions of this French Visitandine and eventually came to be authorized by the universal Church. Soon after, ecclesial reforms stipulated that visual depictions of the Sacred Heart express a fulsome theology. Henceforth, the heart was not to be publicly displayed except as a component of the entire figure of Jesus.

What is significant here for Catholic spirituality is the observation that Catholic visual images such as the Sacred Heart are richly textured and complex. They are not merely pedagogical, decorative, or descriptive. Neither do they represent and communicate the insights of a single artist. Rather they represent a lengthy and communal process of prayer and theological reflection. They mean all that they have meant in the past, and continue to gather to them the varied meanings gleaned by the people for whom they are sources of wisdom. They are incredibly rich visual symbols of the fullness of the faith.

Exemplary of the creative reception of tradition is Saint Alphonsus de Liguori who in the nineteenth century, fully steeped in the broad currents of the devotion, wrote his own prayerful novena to the Sacred Heart. The novena would typically be prayed before an image of Jesus with his heart exposed on his breast. In his prayer, the founder of the Redemptorist Order explored the immense wealth of spiritual insight that the heart image carried, expanding it further. The novena comprises nine meditations on aspects of the heart: namely that the Heart of Jesus is worthy of our love; it is loving, longs to be loved by us, is sorrowful, is compassionate, is generous, is grateful, nevertheless despised, yet faithful. One selection from this beautiful exposition of the deepest nature of God is presented here:

> Oh that we could realize the love that burns in the heart of Jesus for us! He has loved us to such a degree that if the love of all men and women, the love of all the angels and all the saints were united together they would not be equal to one thousandth part of the love of the heart of Jesus. He has loved us immensely more than we can love ourselves. He has loved us almost to excess. What greater excess could there be than that a God should die for his creatures? He has loved us to the very end: "He loved his own in the world and he loved them to the end" (Jn 13:1). There has never been a moment from all eternity in which our God has not thought of us and loved each one of us: "With age old love I have loved you; so I have kept my mercy toward you" (Jer 31:3). For love of us he became man and chose a life of suffering, ending with death on the Cross. He has loved us more than his own honor, his own comfort, more even than his own life since he sacrificed all these to show us the extent of his love for us. Is not this, in fact, an

excess of love which must fill with amazement the very angels of heaven for all eternity? It is this very same love which has prompted him to remain with us in the Most Blessed Sacrament, as on a throne of love. He remains there motionless under the appearance of a little bread in the Ciborium, without any external signs of his divine majesty, and with apparently no other purpose than to demonstrate his love for us all.

Love makes us wish to be in the presence of the one we love. It is this love which makes Jesus Christ remain with us in the Blessed Sacrament. His thirty-three years on this earth were insufficient for him to demonstrate his love for us and so his desire to be with us led him to perform the greatest of all his miracles, namely, the institution of the Holy Eucharist...This love for us has led him to become the food of our souls, to unite himself with us so that our hearts and his would become one and the same...This love is a truth of faith totally beyond my comprehension. O love of Jesus, make yourself known to us and loved in return!

"NOVENA TO THE SACRED HEART"
ALPHONSUS DE LIGUORI: SELECTED WRITINGS

The story of the Sacred Heart did not end with Margaret Mary's visions or with Alphonsus' novena, but it did become the symbol of the Catholic faith until the Second Vatican Council. In the modern era, the Church faced many challenges. And the history of the use of the image of the Sacred Heart is a complex one, changing with shifting political, cultural, and ecclesial waters. The devotion has taken many forms, some of which may seem outdated today. Nevertheless, the spiritual power of the image remains and perhaps may once again take new life in the hearts and minds of a new generation.

MUSIC AND PRAYER

We have made reference in this discussion of prayer to the texts of hymns and canticles that we encounter, especially in liturgy. But it is not only the text of hymns that warrant our attention, but the music and the realization of the music. A favorite saying of choir masters and choristers is one attributed to Saint Augustine: *Qui cantat, bis orat.* ("The one who sings prays twice.") What this suggests is that singing, and by extension the making of music, can be a practice of prayer. Clearly, just as all study, all visual imagery, all speech, and all thought are not necessarily prayer but may be actualized in a way that becomes prayer, all music, even if performed in church, is not necessarily prayer. Music may be simply performed competently or even beautifully and be basically about the performer. Or music may be the vehicle that carries the heart to God. The Psalms, which are the central songs of the Church's liturgies, are full of references to song and music used for generations as God's people have brought their praise, lament, and thanksgiving before the Lord.

Plain chant (sometimes called Gregorian chant) is one of the traditional modes of Catholic musical expression.

Plain chant is generally unaccompanied and monophonic rather then polyphonic (employing many tones or voices). Cultivated in western monastic liturgy, plain chant was for centuries the characteristic Catholic music, enjoying periodic revivals between eras of diminished use. Some Catholic churches today have increased the use of plain chant, with the hope that the modal, haunting beauty of the chant might aid in reflective worship.

Other types of church music may conduce to a prayer experience, both for music ministers and for congregational participants. If people have worshipped for a lifetime through the modality of traditional hymns, those melodies are deeply entwined with a lived sense of the presence of God. Contemporary music also provides people with a repertoire of melodic memories, through which the experience of the mystery at the heart of all is recalled. The use of music as prayer has been part of the human experience of encounter with the Divine. Certainly music is liberally employed today in retreat settings, faith sharing groups, and personal prayer. Indeed, gentle instrumental music often helps to move listeners out of the linear left brain dominance of much of ordinary life into an open place in the self, where feelings, intuition, creativity, and vulnerability may allow one to meet God. Beginning a personal session of prayer with recorded music or entering into prayer with a song helps to mark off the space and atmosphere of prayer from the hustle, harshness, and anxieties that we often bring with us from our daily activities.

Prayerful music does not necessarily have to be slow

or restrained. Catholicism is a global communion, and the American Church contains within it many diverse cultural expressions. One need only go to one of the thousands of United States parishes where Las Mañanitas is celebrated on December twelfth, the feast of Our Lady of Guadalupe, to hear the singing. The Virgin, beloved of Catholics of Mexican heritage as well as countless others, is "awakened" on her feast day by those who love her. The songs carry the hearts of her devotees to a realm of "flowers and song," beauty, comfort, and hope:

Que Linda esta la mañana en que vengo saludarte,
venimos todos con gusto y placer a felicitarte
El día en que tú naciste nacieron todas las flores,
Y en la pila de bautismo cantaron los ruiseñores
Ya viene amaneciendo ya la luz del día nos dio,
levántate Virgencita, mira que ya amaneció
De las estrellas del cielo tengo que barjarte dos:
Una para saludarte y otra para decirte adiós
Ya viene alboreando el día; Que linda esta la mañana,
Saludemos a Maria, Buenos días, Guadalupana.

MAÑANITAS TAPATÍAS

How beautiful is the morning when I come
to greet you
We all come with joy to congratulate you
The day you were born all the flowers were born
Nightingales sang in the baptismal font
The daylight is dawning

Rise, little Virgin, look it is already morning
I will take two stars from heaven
One to greet you, one to say goodbye
Dawn is already breaking
Let us greet Mary, Good morning, dear Guadalupe.

Ardent and expressive song was the spiritual center of Sister Thea Bowman's life and ministry. A member of the Franciscan Sisters of Perpetual Adoration of LaCrosse, Wisconsin, Sister Thea brought to her chosen Catholic faith the knowledge that music was a powerful spiritual medium. A religious seeker at a young age, Thea was nurtured in the Episcopal, Methodist, and Baptist traditions before finding her spiritual home in Roman Catholicism in 1947. But she brought with her not only her ecumenical experience but her experiences as an African American that had nurtured her on the spiritual path of black music. A gifted singer herself, Sister Thea also taught, gave retreats, and wrote about music, especially the spirituals she learned at her grandparents' knees. "Each spiritual is in its own way a prayer," she would write, "of yearning or celebration, of praise, petition, or contemplation, a simple lifting of heart, mind, voice, and life to God" (*Sister Thea Bowman, Shooting Star*). She taught that praying the spirituals that had emerged out of the faith crucible of an enslaved people could lead anyone deeper into the divine embrace. "Dem Bones," "Deep River," "Go Down Moses," "Go Where I Send Thee," and "Were You There?" were all part of the sung legacy of the vibrant tradition of prayer from which Thea Bowman drew. In *Sister Thea: Songs of My People*, she set forth a practice for using these spirituals that was rich in tradition and could engage a practitioner at the deepest level:

1. Choose a place of quiet and reflection. Shut out distractions.
2. Gently move with the music. Let it calm your body. Let yourself become engaged, participatory, involved. Make a conscious effort to work your way into a mode of prayer that combines thought, memory, imagination, and bodily response, that demands action in the real world of every day.
3. Concentrate on the words of the song and the scriptural images they invoke. Concentrate your energies. Engage your mind, your Biblical memory, your memory of your own experiences of life and of God. Engage your imagination. See and hear and feel, taste and touch the Biblical reality. See it all in living color. Let the words and music speak to your whole soul, to your feelings, passions, and emotions. Feel what it means to have walked dry-shod through the Reed Sea, to have placed your firstborn child in a manger, to have sat with Jesus by a well in Samaria, to have watched Jesus nailed upon a cross.
4. Pray with the song. Feel God's presence. Contemplate his goodness. Celebrate the Biblical theme in relationship to the daily mystery of God's working in your own life. Celebrate your own faith and hope and love. Pray in your own way. Move peacefully and gently as you feel drawn to discursive meditation or affective prayer or the contemplative prayer of simple resting in union with God.

5. Pray the spirituals from time to time with family and friends. Pray the spirituals from time to time in liturgy.

SONGS OF MY PEOPLE,
QUOTED IN *SISTER THEA BOWMAN: SHOOTING STAR*

WRITING AS PRAYER

Other types of prayer in the context of the current United States have become common, ecumenically-practiced ways of prayer. Sometimes popular contemporary ways to pray are practiced in self-development or psychological circles as well. For example, keeping a journal is a mode of paying attention to the divine presence in one's daily life or a means of communicating one's thoughts directly to God through journaling. This has become a popular contemporary spiritual discipline for many Catholics. Today there are workshops in journaling that may be offered under the auspices of various psychologists, as a tool for ongoing self-growth.

Spiritual writing, of course, is not new and is not simply an aid to psychological growth. Journaling can be a profound Catholic mode of prayer. We have the recorded writings of many saints and spiritual masters of the past. In fact, the way we know of those masters is often through their writings. Some of these writings may have originated as preached sermons, instructional treatises, descriptions of experiences meant to edify others, and so forth. But other writings originated as private or not so private conversations with God. Many of the poems of twentieth century English Catholic spiritual writer Caryll Houselander had their genesis in her personal diaries. Dorothy Day, the American foundress of the

Catholic Worker Movement, was a daily diarist who kept a record of her inner life, as well as her intimate reflections on the urban ministry to the marginalized that was her life's work. Noted spiritual writer Thomas Merton was another one of this group whose spiritual practice included keeping a journal. For all of these figures, as for many Catholics today, journaling can be a means of paying attention to the way in which God is present in one's life.

At the head of this group of Catholics whose writing is also spiritual practice is Saint Augustine of Hippo, author of the legendary Confessions, which historians cite as the first autobiography in the western canon and which inspired generations of others to put pen to paper. A contemporary exemplar of this mode of spiritual practice is Benedictine sister Macrina Wiederkehr, who has spent many years of her contemplative journey working her way to God through the art of writing poetry. Attentive to the autumns, winters, springs, and summers near her monastery in Fort Smith, Arkansas; to the rhythmic seasons of the liturgical year, and to the changing seasons of her own spiritual life, Wiederkehr has crafted poems that weave these intertwining seasonal experiences into a lovely literary tapestry, which she offers to others as a guide to prayer.

STUDY AS PRAYER

It should be noted that in the Catholic tradition, the intellectual life—the pursuit of knowledge—is very much a part of the spiritual quest. This has long been the case. In the Benedictine tradition, prayer and study are two of the central components of a monk's life. The late Benedictine scholar Jean LeClercq coined the phrase, "the love of learning and the desire for God" as descriptive of the heart of the Benedictine enterprise. But it is not only the monk who pursues knowledge of God through study. Some people will be called, like Jacob with the angel (Genesis 32), to wrestle in a formal manner with the great questions that faith poses. The theologian has an important and distinctive role to play in nurturing the faith alongside the bishop, priest, catechist, preacher, spiritual director, and pastoral minister. But it is not only those who experience calls such as these who can and should find spiritual sustenance in study. When one loves something or someone, it is natural to want to know them more deeply.

The Catholic tradition has never been anti-intellectual, but has encouraged study as a way of deepening intimacy with God. And it has not only been the study of Scripture or theology that has been encouraged, but the arts, history, languages, and social sciences as well, these disciplines give us insight into humankind and God's created world. French Jesuit paleontologist Pierre Teilhard de Chardin, whose intimate knowledge of the amethyst, citrine, and chalcedony of his native Auvergne and of the flora and fossils of Egypt where he was sent as a young teacher, led to his startling mature vision of a cosmic evolution originating and culminating in the heart of Christ. Teilhard's religious-scientific vision was such that he perceived the geologic world itself as a divine milieu. One also thinks of modern theologians like Karl Rahner and Hans Urs von Balthazar, who not only contributed to the development of Catholic theology, but whose writings on prayer and worship reveal a deep contemplative practice that sustained their intellectual pursuits. Study, as important as it is, should always go hand in hand with worship and faith. It can thus become its own hymn of praise to the One who created humankind in the divine image and likeness.

4. Practices of Discernment

It is commonplace in spiritual teaching to insist that, while each person's relationship with God is deeply personal, we are not always objective interpreters of our own experience. Since spirituality is essentially about growth and transformation, we should be in conversation with others in order to gain new perspectives and to be guided in seeing where God is moving us forward into new life. Franciscan Damien Isabel has suggested there are several concentric circles of guidance available to us in the Church community, and if we avail ourselves of these, we can respond with more alacrity to the Spirit's promptings. The first circle is the wider tradition, which includes the Scriptures, theology, ethics, liturgy, and the writings of the spiritual masters and other wise teachers, past and present. Then there is the circle of the local community, the gathered church where one prays. Inside this circle are smaller faith groupings such as ongoing prayer groups, directed or preached retreat experiences, Cursillo, World Youth Day and Marriage Encounter, or faith based social justice volunteer experiences. Inside this circle are one-on-one or small group spiritual direction opportunities. Farther still inside this circle are spiritual friendships.

The point here is that there are a variety of guides available to us as we seek to walk the Way. Central to that walk is the ability to discern the promptings of the Spirit who guides us. It is surely clear to most people that we are influenced by any number of "voices" coming from many directions. We are shaped by the surrounding culture which tends to tell us what is important and who we should be. Some of this is wholesome: we may need to listen to the medical community in order to pay better attention to our health. Some of it is not: emulating celebrities or living beyond one's means to impress the neighbors is counterproductive. We also may absorb the prejudices, penchant for violence, and destructive attitudes we are bombarded with in blogs, on radio, TV, and the Internet. We hear the voices of our families. Some of this is also wholesome: we may have been loved and nurtured well. Some of it may not be: we may have been physically or psychologically abused and our perspectives stunted as a result. Inside ourselves, we are often like a multi-channeled stereo system, with too many conflicting desires, thoughts, feelings, opinions, hopes, dreams, and fears.

SPIRITUAL GUIDANCE

One of the most ancient arts of the spiritual life is the art of discerning between these many voices in order to detect the texture and sound of God's Spirit. It is possible to learn this art oneself, or at least become attuned, but availing oneself of guidance is also necessary. As suggested, the larger tradition is the widest circle in which this occurs. And local faith communities, as well as smaller intentional communities, are very important in helping to nurture sensitivity to the

Spirit. Many folks today, however, are drawn to the even more specific practice of spiritual direction. This one-on-one (or small group) practice involves a visit with a trained and/ or experienced spiritual director who helps a person listen to the way in which God is active in his or her life, suggests prayer practices, or helps that person to see the resistance to the divine initiative. Spiritual direction is not to be conflated with therapy, pastoral counseling, or theological instruction. These are cognate ministries of which someone might want to avail themselves. But spiritual direction, while it concerns itself with the whole of life, focuses primarily on a person's relationship with God and the way that relationship manifests itself in daily life.

There is a great deal of interest in spiritual guidance today, and a few comments to help clarify the nature of the ministry are in order. Spiritual guidance is an ancient Christian art. Its origins are generally traced to the desert dwellers of Egypt, Syria, and Palestine, among whom some were recognized as gifted spiritual teachers. These men and women were self-authenticating in the sense that the transformation of their lives, achieved through grace and ascetic discipline, was evident to those around them. These holy ones attracted followers who sought them out in order to be formed into the new persons promised in the Gospels; the relationship that grew between master and disciple in this context was enduring. Through his or her hard-earned knowledge of the human heart and its complexity, the master guided a disciple to deeper self-knowledge and self-emptying in order for the new person to come into being.

In these early times, spiritual guidance was not linked to any ecclesial role: most of the desert luminaries were laity. Eventually, as the desert impulse was institutionalized in monasticism, spiritual guidance was exercised within the monastery, either by community leaders or by elders who were regarded as having a gift for discerning spirits and reading hearts. Over the long centuries, spiritual guidance became increasingly identified with vowed religious life, and even in the early modern period, it was seen as a function of the priesthood.

The priest-confessor model of spiritual guidance hails from the sixteenth through the nineteenth centuries. Gradually, however, the idea of spiritual guidance as a distinct charism or gift that may or may not be given along with ordination surfaced once again. Trained spiritual guidance today is offered by lay persons, as well as by some religious women and some priests. From the earliest Christian era, the discernment of spirits was viewed as a spiritual gift, bestowed on some, rather than as part of holding a specific office or of following a certain lifestyle. That is also true today. A reputable director should be familiar with the ecumenical sweep of Christianity. However, an individual may often feel more at home with a guide whose tradition is his or her own.

So why and how might one seek a spiritual guide today? As suggested, direction is not pastoral counseling, theological instruction, or therapy; for those needs, one should seek a priest, pastoral minister, counselor, therapist, or theology instructor. A person who seeks spiritual direction today may be seeking to deepen his relationship with God, or he may want to negotiate some key life transition in which he wishes to be led by God's prompting, rather than by conventional expectations. He or she may be considering a vocation to marriage or religious life, or feel drawn to service to others and need help discerning a future direction in a prayerful manner. The individual may wish to learn to pray, or to pray more generously. A life crisis or relationship issue may present the occasion for a new look at one's self in relation to God and the ultimate values one professes. The reasons are legion for seeking out a guide.

In looking for a director, it is good to know that prudence is in order. One might seek recommendations from a pastoral minister or consult the list put out by Spiritual Directors International, which, while not a recommendation for a given director, can help find those who identify themselves as spiritual guides in a particular region. Since spiritual guidance is a gift, spiritual direction is not simply a profession in which one takes a few courses and hangs up a shingle. Nevertheless, more and more training programs that help to hone the gift are springing up around the country. This enables spiritual guides to be aware of the various dimensions of their ministry, to learn how to identify a directee who may need to be referred to some other helping professional, and to avoid practices that may be detrimental. There are also persons in religious orders who have training in direction, in the sense that they have been involved in the formation of community members.

It is helpful to do some research about the background, training, and experience of a person identifying himself as a spiritual guide. In some contexts, spiritual direction is offered for free: a parish, retreat house, or university may have a resident guide. Or some sort of fee may be requested. The negotiation of a fee is likely one of the initial topics to be discussed. Spiritual directors will always encourage a directee to determine, over the first several meetings, whether the relationship is beneficial. Those who seek spiritual direction have the freedom and personal responsibility to make their own choices or change guides according to their needs.

The goal of spiritual guidance is ultimately the spiritual freedom of the one seeking guidance. It is not about a set instructional program or the agenda of the director. Indeed, while the term "director" is the one most commonly used, today many engaged in the ministry prefer the image of a companion or a midwife, images which stress the fact that in spiritual guidance, God is the true "director." While the direction relationship is generally not coldly formal, neither should it have the informality of a friendship. And while professional and ethical competence may be expected of a director, a directee should never feel that he or she is simply there to receive "professional" advice. Sessions, which typically last an hour or so and are spaced several weeks apart, focus on the directee's story and faith journey. While a director may, on occasion, contribute a personal anecdote, the sharing is not mutual. A person should feel free to assess the fruitfulness of the enterprise at any time. Discernment is at the heart of the direction relationship: the movement and prompting of the Divine, as the directee is gently reshaped and formed by the breath of God.

DISCERNING DESIRE

As with the topic of spiritual guidance, this discussion of discernment is general and is not meant to be prescriptive. Indeed, a great deal of further exploration and prayer is needed to sort out what God is doing in one's life, and to what one is being called. But there are several themes connected with discernment that should be mentioned. The first of these is the experience of consolation and desolation as guiding principles in discernment. Saint Ignatius of Loyola, founder of the Jesuits, was a master of self-observation. He developed a rather extensive system of discernment based on tradition and his own experience, which became the basis for the teachings in his Spiritual Exercises. The wisdom from the Exercises, an intensive process of formation, has been passed on through the Jesuit Order and those persons beyond the order who are formed in the Ignatian tradition. Ignatius believed that one could attend carefully to movements of consolation and desolation as markers for identifying the Spirit.

One story will suffice to get a flavor of this process. Ignatius, a sixteenth-century nobleman from the Basque country, directed his early life according to society's expectations. He was a "ladies' man" and a dashing soldier, intent on glory and fame. His life was interrupted when he was severely wounded in battle and confined to bed in a country castle. Ignatius was used to reading chivalric romances, which egged him on to conquests of all sorts, but the occupants of the castle could only supply him with Ludolph of Saxony's *Life of Christ* and de Voragine's medieval book on the lives of the saints to pass the time. Soon he discovered something interesting. He was used to being enthused while reading the romances, but when he finished them, he felt empty and dissatisfied. His experience reading the sacred books was the opposite. He found himself enthused with the drama and heroism in them. That sensibility continued, even when he had finished reading. Something important was drawing him in a new way. His former attractions were fleeting, ultimately meaningless, while the new ones had permanence. Ignatius went on to develop his methods of discernment, methods which have survived the test of time. Put much too simply, Ignatius observed that for persons who were not already walking with God, those mired in sin or unaware of God's call to them, the "good" spirit was disturbing; it felt like water on a rock. The "evil" spirit (not of God) felt pleasurable and seductive. The opposite was true for people already embarked on the Way: the "good" spirit consoled; it felt peaceful, like water on a sponge. The "evil" spirit was agitated and caused desolation. Today these general principles of consolation and desolation still form the backbone of the art of Ignatian discernment. (It is important to note that what are referred to are not fleeting feelings like the ones that come and go at a moment's notice nor moods induced by illness, lack of sleep, or personal preferences.)

DISCERNMENT AND THE DARK NIGHT OF THE SOUL

Another approach to the discernment of spirits was also articulated in the sixteenth century, this time by Saint John of the Cross, the reformer of the male branch of the Carmelite

Order. John is famous for his great spiritual treatises, among them, *The Ascent of Mount Carmel* and *Dark Night of the Soul*. One of John's contributions to the tradition of discernment was to identify some of the signs that indicate a person is moving from more typical sorts of prayer into a prayer that leads beyond words, feelings, and thoughts. Additionally, he was a master at describing the ways in which some individuals are drawn into deeper intimacy with God through unknowing rather than knowing. The observation of this early modern Spaniard is that the Way may be characterized by the often destabilizing process of stripping or letting go in every aspect of experience. Not only does following Christ involve a purification of the sensate dimensions of life, but the spiritual as well. Some of this we effect ourselves, through the spiritual disciplines. Some of it is effected by God. Some of the stripping is exterior, some interior. The dark nights of which John writes so eloquently are not to be equated with clinical depression or physical or psychological illness, nor necessarily with aridity in prayer. Rather they are part of the mysterious process of passionate love that some individuals experience and which results in being conformed more closely to Christ.

For the Carmelite saint, three stages of the life of serious prayer—which correspond to the classic pattern of purgation, illumination, and union—can be described. The first is the stage of beginners who practice discursive meditation and whose prayer is centered on the sensory self (external things and the use of imagination and memory). The second stage is the stage of proficients who have progressed to contemplative prayer and the spiritual self. (The external and internal senses are quieted in order to receive God's self-communication.) The third stage is of those perfected, those wholly transformed and in union with God. As this process progresses, the one praying moves deeper and deeper into levels of stripping or letting go. First, sensory satisfaction in prayer dries up. All those consoling, warm feelings give way to dryness and aridity. This inaugurates a period which John calls the dark night of the senses. The individual is unable to pray in the way to which he or she was accustomed, nor does this person derive any emotional satisfaction from the spiritual quest. Nevertheless, as confusing and painful as this is, the person still desires ardently to continue on the way. God is beginning to communicate God's self more directly to that person, thus leaving the senses and exterior self empty and dry. Gradually the one who progresses further begins to sense a gentle, subtle presence, and prayer becomes more nondiscursive. Over a number of years, this sort of prayer transforms the individual's way of being in the world. Another phase, which John terms the "Dark Night of the Spirit," takes place for some people. This night is filled with interior pain and disorientation. The one who prays sees more clearly the disorder of his life and may experience alienation from self, others, and God. The God he or she has known and loved seems to have disappeared. The cause of this pain, according to the Carmelite, is the bright light of God's self-communication. Cherished but ultimately false images of self and of God must be abandoned. A sort of spiritual death occurs. The Dark Night of Spirit ends when the individual becomes truly centered in God, and the alternating visions of God's goodness juxtaposed to his or her own disorder cease. In both of these Dark Nights, the sensory and the spiritual, disordered attachments are purged. God in God's own self, not the consolations of God or our spiritual accomplishment, nor our previous conceptions of ourselves or of God, remains.

The patterns of discernment outlined by John of the Cross are classic. But not all persons experience God's presence in these ways. And, as suggested, some people may be genuinely drawn by God's own Spirit into deep union through visual, discursive, meditative, and embodied forms of prayer. Nevertheless, the Carmelite insight into dark nights is an important part of the Catholic tradition. As suggested, spiritual discernment, especially at times of decision, transition, crisis, or deep confusion, is best done within the circles of guidance of the faith community. Clearly, interior movements such as the dark nights need to be carefully discerned. One may, in fact, be clinically depressed or experiencing relational or personal difficulties which would call for some other type of consultation. But even for the daily routine of our lives, there is a bottom line when we either seek the Way among the many ways one might travel, or determine whether we are faithful followers. Any action, thought, relationship, decision, or path that is Christian will eventually lead to greater faith, love, and hope. Any given step along the way may be unclear, any fork in the road bewildering, any eventuality arduous, even heartbreaking. But in the end, the flowering of faith, love, and hope are the long term tests of any discernment of Spirits.

5. Companions on the Way

The Second Vatican Council clearly enunciated the idea that all of us, not only the canonized saints, are called to live holy lives. The Universal Call to Holiness, as it is referred to, asserts that it is through our baptisms into the Mystical Body that we are incorporated into the holiness that is Christ's. But our baptismal incorporation is only the beginning. We are constantly called throughout our lives to respond ever more generously to God's encouraging Spirit which, in the words of the liturgical sequence we pray at Pentecost, consoles, refreshes, warms, gifts, enlightens, cleanses, and guides. In some sense, all that we have discussed thus far is about sanctification, becoming holy. The spiritual life is about holiness, but not a "plaster of paris," conventional holy card type of holiness. Often people think of holiness as other-worldly or as something that only the saints possess. True, we believe that the saints manifest holiness to an extraordinary degree. But the charge to live into the depth and breadth of God's merciful love and to extend something of that love to others is not simply the responsibility of the canonized saints. It is all of ours.

We have suggested that the guidance of the wider faith community is essential for the practice of discernment. We would also suggest that the regular company one keeps is an important part of growing in love of God and neighbor. To grow in faith, hope and love, one must be in the company of those who are likewise seeking to grow. While silence and solitude are important mediums through which we may mature, they should not be environments that isolate or shield us from the salutary learnings that others offer us. We grow in grace, both by being enriched by the knowledge and wisdom of others, and by experiencing the challenging growth that often comes though human relationships. Formation happens not only alongside but through others who are also traveling the Way.

There are many ways to seek out the company of others traveling the Way. Diocesan or Catholic college or university-based programs of study and reflection may help one's faith to mature. Parishes may sponsor faith sharing or prayer groups and provide opportunities for parochial spiritual nurture. Other sorts of intentional formation communities are important as well. Participation in an Ignatian Christian Life Community, in a Benedictine Oblate program, a Third Order Franciscan community, in one of the many International Associations of the Faithful for laity, in the Personal Prelature of Opus Dei, in a Secular Institute, or one of the many associate groups attached to other religious communities, all can provide the context through which focused spiritual formation occurs. The recent flourishing of lay associate programs sponsored by religious orders and congregations has been, in fact, one of the most striking features of the contemporary American Church landscape. Studies carried out in 2000 and 2005 by the Center for Applied Research in the Apostolate and the North American Conference of Associates and Religious indicated that, of the reporting congregations (and not all religious communities were surveyed), there were an estimated twenty-eight thousand associates who were sharing in the mission and the charism of established religious institutes.

Another way in which we may grow in grace in the company of others is through the gift of spiritual friendship. Our culture tends to minimize the importance of friendships. We often consider friends less important than those we say we love: parents, children, spouses. We relegate the term "friend" to colleagues, sports buddies, or pleasant but uncommitted fellowship. In the classic tradition, friendship is seen as a form of love which, it will be remembered, has its source and end in God. Friendship is a distinctive love that must, by definition, be mutual (it has to go both ways) and equal (true friends must be capable of identifying with and desiring the good for each other).

Clearly, not all friendships are rightly described as spiritual friendships. But some are. Twelfth century Cistercian writer Aelred of Rievaulx penned a treatise, *On Spiritual Friendship*, that remains edifying today. In it, Aelred speaks of the power of a truly life-giving relationship with God at its center. A spiritual friend can be a mirror, a challenge, an inspiration, a mentor, and a confidant. True spiritual friendship is not possessive or exploitative, nor does it ask anything that might diminish another. It is a graced relationship through which we are more clearly conformed to the divine image and likeness.

Five centuries after Aelred, Saint Francis de Sales continued to reflect on the formative value of spiritual friendship:

The higher the virtues you share and exchange with others, the more perfect your friendship will be. If this participation is in matters of knowledge, the resulting friendship is certainly very praiseworthy. It is still more so if you have virtues in common, namely, prudence, temperance, fortitude, and justice. If your mutual and reciprocal exchanges concern charity, devotion, and Christian perfection, O God, how precious this friendship will be! It will be excellent because it comes from God, excellent because it leads to God, excellent because its bond will endure eternally in God. How good it is to love here on earth as they love in heaven and to learn to cherish one another in this world as we shall do eternally in the next!

INTRODUCTION TO THE DEVOUT LIFE

Saint Francis considers these friendships to be of such spiritual benefit that he expounds on the subject for six chapters. Spiritual friendships, whether they are one-on-one or shared by a small group, may last for years or enter one's life for a season. They are one of the pathways by which the Spirit pries open hearts so that we might mature. The point is that we are deeply influenced by those with whom we spend time. If we are surrounded and nurtured by persons who take the process of faith formation seriously, persons who have the humility, courage, and willingness to be challenged and remade, to risk the adventure of the spiritual life, we too may change, be remade, become more what God intended us to be. Holiness cannot be identified with a series of propositions, a fixed set of ideas, or conventional actions. There is no generic holiness, only the mystery of divine energy working through a particular personality in a specific time, place, and circumstance. Holiness is Love in action in all its spaciousness, graciousness, and capacity to surprise.

6. Practices of Presence

The sixty-third Psalm gives voice to one of the deepest of human longings, the longing for intimacy with the Divine.

> *O God, you are my God—*
> *for you I long!*
> *For you my body yearns;*
> *for you my soul thirsts,*
> *Like a land parched, lifeless,*
> *and without water.*
>
> PSALM 63:2

THE REAL PRESENCE

Catholic spirituality incorporates this most human of longings. First, it affirms that our persistent desire to be present to God is answered by a divine response in time and space, even though God in God's fullness is beyond temporal and spatial confines. In actuality, God first longs for us, and we then respond in kind. The doctrine of the Real Presence in the Eucharist is at the heart of this affirmation. Christ is offered to us not only once, in history, but continually in the host. Para-liturgical practices have grown over the centuries to honor the fact that God is truly present in the sacrament. In eucharistic adoration, the consecrated host is displayed in a monstrance, and the faithful are invited to be present in silent adoration and prayer. Benediction of the Blessed Sacrament is generally observed as a service in which formal prayers and hymns are offered, typically the ancient chant, *Tantum Ergo* ("Come adore this wondrous presence"). It consists of the last verses of *Pange Lingua*, ("Hail our Savior's Glorious Body"). This astonishing gift has been the focus of many devotional writings, among them this one penned by Saint Alphonsus de Liguori in the eighteenth century:

> Jesus knew that his hour had come to pass from this world to the father. He loved his own in the world and he loved them to the end" (Jn 13:1). Knowing that the time had come for him to leave this earth and that he was soon to die for us, our loving savior wished to leave us the greatest gift his love could give, the gift of the most holy sacrament. St. Bernardino of Siena says that those tokens of love which are given at death remain firmly engraved on the memory and are the most treasured. People on their death bed often make a last bequest of an article of clothing or a ring to their friends as a token of their affection. But you, Jesus, as you were on the point of leaving this world, what was the token of love that you left us? It was not an article of clothing or a ring, but your body and your blood,

your soul and divinity, your whole self. As St. John Chrysostom expresses it: "He gave you everything, he left himself nothing.

"THE PRACTICE OF THE LOVE OF JESUS,"
ALPHONSUS DE LIGUORI: SELECTED WRITINGS

The acknowledgment of the gift of the Real Presence points to the importance of presence in the Catholic imagination. God inclines to us, welcoming human intimacy. And we, in turn, draw near.

SILENCE, SOLITUDE, AND SABBATH OBSERVANCE

The contemplative has nothing to tell you except to reassure you and say that if you dare to penetrate your own silence and risk the sharing of that solitude with the lonely other who seeks God through you, then you will truly recover the light and the capacity to understand what is beyond words and beyond explanations because it is too close to be explained: it is the intimate union in the depths of your own heart, of God's spirit and your own secret inmost self...

THE HIDDEN GROUND OF LOVE

American spiritual writer Thomas Merton, in a "message from contemplatives to the world" that had been requested by Pope Paul VI in 1967, wrote in a fresh way about some of the most traditional of spiritual practices, namely the silence and solitude through which we may draw near to God. It may seem counterintuitive to think of silence as facilitating intimacy, but that is the consistent claim of the spiritual masters of the tradition. "Be still and know that I am God," Scripture proclaims. Silence creates a clearing in our minds so that our hearing can become acute. We learn to listen, we learn to wait, we learn to hush our restless, busy selves and attend to what God might long to say to us. The silence that punctuates Catholic worship, and which allows the Word or our reception of the Eucharist to truly be taken in, is only one example of the practice of silence in the tradition. Monastic practice incorporates silence, not periodically, but as the habitual backdrop against which true hearing can take place. Discernment too is facilitated by entry into silence. Its gifts are twofold. First, silence enables us to be free of the cultural noise that keeps us from listening to our own hearts. Additionally, silence is the medium through which our internal noise becomes audible and the medium through which we eventually come to identify the whisper of the Spirit.

Catholic retreat houses frequently offer silent retreats or encourage time spent in silence during preached retreats or spirituality programs. The quiet of Marian grottos or shrines invite prayer and reflection. And private practices of silent, wordless prayer, of simply allowing oneself to be in the divine presence, are often graced times. Silence is a medium that, if cultivated, can lead us deeper into the mystery of the divine life. The practice of exterior silence allows us to cultivate inner stillness and ultimately to begin to plumb the profound silence that is at the heart of the divine life itself, a silence that is a language all its own.

Solitude is a related counterintuitive practice that may

facilitate an experience of divine presence. When we are alone with God, we are, of course, in fact less alone than at any other time. But we do need opportunities to withdraw periodically to gain perspective on our lives. The wonderful or vexing people who surround us daily may tend to define us. We may have few chances for self-reflection. Too often our lives consist of doing, going, and striving. Intentional solitude dehabituates us from our familiar selves and opens up new possibilities for growth, discovery, and insight. When we become truly present to ourselves in solitude, we become capable of authentic encounter with God.

The Catholic landscape for millennia has been intentionally dotted with solitary spaces. Certain cultural and geographical parts of our tradition have been especially sensitive to the need for solitude in the quest for divine intimacy: for example, the remote islands off the coasts of Ireland and Scotland have been for centuries the solitary sites of Celtic Catholic spiritual practice. Even in America, there are places set aside for solitude. For example, on the remote coast of Big Sur in northern California and in the countryside outside Bloomingdale, Ohio, the ancient Camaldolese hermit order makes space for the serious spiritual pilgrim in their small cells. Many retreat facilities or other monastic foundations may provide hermitages or rooms set apart for solitude. Some may offer opportunities for silent retreats, either done on one's own or in concert with periodic meetings with a spiritual guide.

One other practice of presence related to silence and solitude is the practice of Sabbath-keeping. Catholics are certainly accustomed to attending Mass on Sundays, but perhaps have not always given a lot of thought to the spiritual art of Sabbath-keeping in a broader way. The biblical injunction to honor the Sabbath and keep it holy is not simply about attendance at worship, but about the cultivation of a Sabbath sensibility, a sense of time set aside to honor God, to inhabit time as a spacious gift rather than as something to be filled up or fleeting. In the Scriptures, Sabbath-keeping is linked to two other intentional temporal ideas: sabbatical and jubilee (Leviticus 25). If biblical Sabbath-keeping is a weekly observance in which work ceases, a sabbatical is the periodic practice of letting land lay fallow and allowing the earth to regenerate itself. Jubilee is the seven-times-seven years (or every fifty years) practice of redistribution of land, forgiveness of debts, and release of captives. We are not sure that ancient Israel ever did observe a jubilee, but wise farming practices necessitated letting some fields lie unplanted to ensure continued productivity, and Israel was devoted to its once a week setting aside of ordinary labor in order to praise and rejoice in what has been called "eternity in time."

Catholics of two generations ago were familiar with the idea of ceasing manual work on the Lord's Day. Our seven day week, twenty-four hour day, producing and consuming culture has tended to overtake our Sabbath-keeping. Recently the notion of reclaiming this ancient wisdom has resurfaced in Catholic circles. The idea is to reconsider how we inhabit time, how we make space for honoring the life we have been given, allowing ourselves to regenerate, and perhaps even radically reorder things so that forgiveness, reconciliation, and redistribution might occur in our own lives. What might it mean to be intentional about staying home with family one evening a week or taking one day a month to simply be with God or going on retreat once a year? What might it be like to reorder our priorities so that we make time to be present to God and to those who we say are dearest to us? What might it mean to stop doing things as we have been? What might it mean to take the time to experience seriously the biblical mandate: Taste and see that the Lord is good?

PRESENCE TO OTHERS

The Catholic sense of the importance of presence is not only expressed in the doctrine of the Real Presence or through the privileged modalities of silence, solitude, or Sabbath-keeping. Being genuinely present to others is also a cherished part of the spiritual tradition. For centuries, Catholics have viewed the practice of the Works of Mercy as an essential component of a Catholic identity. These are traditionally seen as having two major divisions, the corporal and spiritual. The corporal works of mercy are enumerated as feeding the hungry, clothing the naked, sheltering the homeless, visiting the sick, visiting or ransoming prisoners, and burying the dead. The spiritual works of mercy are instructing the ignorant, counseling the doubtful, admonishing sinners, bearing wrongs patiently, forgiving injuries and offenses, comforting the sorrowful, and praying for the living and the dead. Too often, the differences posited between the "contemplative" and "active" lives have played into the false notion that spirituality is simply about interiority and not about deeds. Nothing could be farther from the truth. The realization of God's boundless love experienced in prayer, in liturgy, in silence, in friendships, in study and reading is intimately connected to the love we show to one another. Love is dynamic—it comes to us and flows through us. The hundreds of years of love of neighbor demonstrated in Catholic hospitals, orphanages, schools and relief organizations as well as the literally thousands of Catholic religious orders and congregations of man and women founded to practice the works of mercy bear evidence of this Catholic sensibility.

Today the Catholic Worker movement, one of the most original of lay Catholic communities, continues explicitly to engage in the works of mercy. Founded in New York during the Great Depression by American journalist Dorothy Day and French peasant philosopher Peter Maurin, the loosely-knit Catholic Worker family today, among other aspects of its diffuse identity, oversees Houses of Hospitality across the country that welcome the homeless and marginalized. The personalist philosophy of the Worker distinguishes it from other sorts of social service agencies in that the marginalized guests are greeted as Christ, not simply as clients or outcasts. The practice of genuine presence is exhibited because both guests and members of the Worker communities generally share life together. This often makes for chaos or at least confusion, with all the characters who show up and the multitude of concerns that end up needing attention. However, as Day wrote in her account of the Catholic Worker movement, "The greatest challenge of the day is: how to bring about a revolution of the heart, a revolution that has to start with each one of us? When we begin to take the lowest place, to wash the feet of others, to love our brothers with that burning love, that passion, which led to the Cross, then we can truly say, 'Now I have begun'"(*Loaves and Fishes*).

Such are the works of mercy: messy, demanding, and yet a means of grace. The twentieth century is filled with Catholic examples of the impulse to practice presence with those in need. The L'Arche movement founded in France by Jean Vanier is one of the most striking. As a young man, Vanier was moved by the plight of persons with intellectual disabilities who were institutionalized or mistreated. His response was to become present to them and to create something new, a shared living experience that brings together people with developmental disabilities and those who assist them. In these unique homes, the abled and the disabled seek to recognize one another's unique value and gifts. The L'Arche community in Clinton, Iowa, is the oldest and the most rural of such communities in the United States. Longtime Clinton L'Arche member Kathy Berken has written movingly about the challenges and graces of being intimately present with disabled adults, which she describes as "a gift from God wrapped in mystery. It's a place where we learn to be downright human" (*Walking on the Rolling Deck: Life on the Ark*). Especially in the L'Arche community, one witnesses the face of Jesus who dwelled among the outcasts of society.

It is not only the traditional works of mercy that underscore Catholic practices of presence to others, but the more recent Catholic social teaching tradition which dates from the end of the nineteenth century. With its solid grounding in the bedrock Catholic teaching on the common good, Catholic social teaching has encouraged an entire generation of Catholic young people and many of their elders to take to heart the teaching that human beings are created in the divine image and likeness. Thus each person is seen as having intrinsic dignity which must be honored. Whether a person is poor, immigrant, elderly, disabled, unborn, sick, unemployed, homeless, imprisoned, hungry, or otherwise cast aside, Catholic social teaching makes the claim that all are children of God, and that these little, outcast ones are in fact the ones who must be considered first. God's intent is for a just world in which the gifts of all God's children can flourish and enrich the whole. Unjust structures, laws, social conditions, and arrangements that thwart that just world must be addressed. Today across America, volunteer organizations sponsored by religious orders such as the Claretians, Marianists, Jesuits, Passionists, Salesians, and many others or by organizations like Catholic Charities, give young people an opportunity to do direct service. Volunteer opportunities, both international and domestic, include campus and youth ministry, community organization and housing development, education, homeless shelters and soup kitchens, immigrants and refugees, parish ministry, social justice issues, Spanish-speaking ministries, and work with the elderly, the unemployed, people with HIV/AIDS, street youth, abused women and children, the mentally ill, and the developmentally disabled. The projects that young adult volunteers engage in through these Catholic organizations do not simply answer a social need, they serve as profoundly formative environments. Volunteers pray and work together and come to understand more deeply the extent to which their faith sends them out in solidarity and asks them to love as they have been loved: extravagantly and unstintingly.

Exemplary in a different way of the integration of the various practices of presence are the loosely affiliated international communities inspired by Blessed Charles de Foucauld. An ex-soldier, reformed bon vivant, and former monk, Foucauld, after much searching, came to envision a vocation in imitation of the hidden life of Jesus at Nazareth. Moved by the piety of Muslims he encountered in the deserts of North Africa while on campaign, Foucauld eventually took priestly orders and relocated to French-occupied Algeria, identifying himself as a hermit and a (non-proselytizing) missionary. But in the desert, he lived the way he understood Jesus to have lived in his hidden years before his public ministry, unobtrusively going about his ordinary work among ordinary people. Dual practices of presence characterized his life: daily adoration of the real presence of Christ in the Blessed Sacrament and personal presence to the poor and ordinary. Foucauld died in 1918 without realizing his dream of a community in imitation of the life at Nazareth, but years afterward, his ideals bore fruit through others. Today the Little Brothers of Jesus, the Little Sisters of Jesus, the Little Brothers of the Gospel, the Little Sisters of the Gospel, and Jesus Caritas, a fraternity for priests, continue to live this dual practice. Daily contemplative adoration sustains whatever daily work engages Foucauld's heirs. A small group of Little Sisters travels with the circus as seamstresses; others are street vendors among the poor of Latin America; some of the Little Brothers labor as carpenters or hospice workers; and Jesus Caritas affiliates engage in regular priestly ministry, but give special attention to periodic retreats and presence to God in Prayer.

7. Embodied Practices

They are sometimes humorously referred to as "smells and bells," but what is really named in that phrase is the Catholic instinct that the material world is important and powerful; the body, the senses, the whole of the created realm is saturated with the presence of God. Think of Saint Francis of Assisi preaching to the birds or the thousands of pilgrims who daily walk on bloodied knees to the Mexican shrine of Our Lady of Guadalupe, or of the practices of incensing the altar, genuflecting, or fingering rosary beads. Catholic spirituality can involve contemplative stillness, imageless reflection, and visits to solitary sites where one meets God in wordless prayer, but it also has a robust tradition of practices that involve movement, gesture, material objects, and profoundly embodied communal engagement.

SACRED GESTURES

Catholics may not give much thought to the fact that bodily gesture is very much a part of the Catholic repertoire. Making the sign of the cross, genuflecting, kneeling, standing, reaching into the holy water font, bowing the head, processing the aisle and receiving the host in outstretched hand or on the tongue, drinking from the chalice, smelling the incense, and observing silence are all familiar embodied experiences that occur during liturgical prayer or when entering the sanctuary. Familiar as they may be, they speak articulately about how Catholics think of themselves and of God. They say: entering into a church is entering into God's presence. One needs to prepare for that encounter, to symbolically wash away the dross that clings to one in order to be readied for the encounter. One acknowledges with reverent gestures that, as human beings, we are mortal, fragile, and contingent and that a greater mystery than us exists. One silences the heart and mind so that true listening can occur, so that one can say, with the psalmist, "Speak Lord, your servant is listening, you have the words of everlasting life." One kneels and genuflects to acknowledge God's majesty or stands reverently to hear the Word proclaimed.

Sacred gestures not only communicate something to the outside observer; they are meant to change those of us who use them as well. Observing the hushed silence of the sanctuary or adoration chapel teaches us the art of holy listening and allows us to practice attitudes of receptivity. Sharing the bread and wine with the gathered community enacts our "oneness," along with the shared nourishment that comes from an infinite Love willing to sacrifice on our behalf. The common recitation of the Creed is an affirmation of our shared faith and life in the Mystical Body.

These embodied practices are an essential part of the way Catholics relate to one another and to the Divine. But there are many other embodied practices available outside of the liturgy that may facilitate spiritual growth. Among these are fasting; going on pilgrimage; participation in festivals, feasts, commemorations, processions, sacred theater, and novenas; the use of devotional aids like the rosary, scapulars, and other sacramentals.

FASTING

While it is true that the obligatory Friday abstinence, the prohibition of eating and drinking before partaking in the Eucharist, and the Lenten fasts that so defined Catholics before Vatican II are no longer as severe as they once were, nevertheless, the ancient embodied practice of the fast is still very much a part of Catholic experience. Abstinence (no meat) on Fridays in Lent, abstaining from food an hour before approaching the communion table, and the obligation of abstinence and the limit of only one meal on Ash Wednesday and Good Friday are the formal fasts of the Church today. But the deeper significance of fasting, perhaps more clearly signified by the practice of giving something up for Lent, is twofold. Fasting is a discipline which focuses our energies and priorities. It teaches us the difference between what we genuinely need and what we may merely want. Fasting also helps create an empty space which invites divine presence. Some fasting practices may help us be more attentive to personal growth: perhaps we may give up rich desserts or alcohol as a means of being more mindful about caring for the bodies God has given us. Many contemporary practices of fasting are other-oriented and especially relevant in the modern world. In some parishes or schools, a "hunger banquet" may be prepared. In this exercise, participants draw lots to share the food available. Each lot drawn corresponds to a portion equivalent to the percentage of food available to people in various parts of the world today. One participant may draw the portion equivalent to the food normally consumed by someone in rural Africa or in a poor village in Peru. The participant who draws a typical U.S. portion may be surprised to discover that they are allotted up to ten times the portion available to those who are to feast as citizens of the developing world. Another fast being introduced is the technology fast. Our cultural addiction to instant and constant calling, emailing, texting, and Web-surfing may be seen as toxic habits that keep us from being present to the things to which we really do need to attend. Giving these up for a week, a day, or a season may liberate us to attend more to the movement of the Spirit in our world and lives.

Fasting is in part about the cultivation of discipline and self-control but more profoundly, it is about becoming aware of our deeper hunger for God and not filling up the God-shaped hollow at the center of our beings with anything but that which will truly nourish us.

PILGRIMAGE

Catholics are not alone among religious peoples as they go on pilgrimage. Travel to a holy site or a sacred place is part of human religious experience. But among Christians, Catholics have excelled in this embodied practice. We have travel diaries from as early as the fourth century written by earnest Christian pilgrims who journeyed to the Holy Land in order to retrace the footsteps of Christ. Visiting the locales today where Jesus once lived and the story of faith was first played out still compels many. Other sites are holy for Catholics as well. Rome, as the center of the Catholic world, has long been the destination of Catholic pilgrims.

While visiting the city where the pope resides and where so many events in the Church's history occurred is never out of fashion, there have been years when a Roman pilgrimage was a special focus. Such was the year 2000, demarcated a jubilee year by John Paul II. The jubilee pilgrimage included visits to the dozens of the city's ancient churches, including Saint Peter's Basilica. A pilgrimage is never simply an act of tourism; however, it is an outward journey that corresponds to an interior transformation. One leaves one's habituated place (outer and inner) to travel somewhere new, to let go of old ways, to be refashioned by contact with a sacred place, to see afresh, to be healed, to kindle faith. The focus of Jubilee 2000 was reconciliation and hope.

During the Church's first four centuries, the tombs of the first martyrs were visited by crowds of the faithful, and throughout the middle ages, shrines associated with the saints drew pilgrims far and wide. One of the most popular of medieval European pilgrimage destinations was the Shrine of Santiago (Saint James) at Compostela, in northwest Spain. The route is still heavily traveled. The pilgrim roads to Compostella are long and difficult: there is a sense that such a journey requires sacrifice on the part of the pilgrim. In fact, during the middle ages, a pilgrimage was often assigned to a repentant sinner as a means of penance and of reconciling him or her with the community of faith. As suggested, a pilgrimage is more than a tour or a visit. It can be a means of transformation. Inherent in every pilgrimage is the movement away from a familiar place through a series of sacrificial or initiating experiences to arrive at a different, sacred space.

Today, the sites of Marian apparitions are popular Catholic destinations. Lourdes, France (where Mary is said to have appeared in 1858), draws those seeking healing waters. Fatima, Portugal (1917), arrests pilgrims with its message of conversion. Guadalupe, Mexico (1531), attracts millions annually who wish to be in the presence of *la Virgen Morena* and reaffirm her message of maternal protection. Other officially recognized apparitions also draw pilgrims to Belgium (appearance in 1932 at Beauraing and at Banneux in 1933), to Ireland (at Knock in 1879), and to other sites in France (Pontmain in 1871, Paris in 1830, La Salette in 1846). There have been many claims about apparitions of the Virgin made over the centuries. In general, Church authorities are very cautious about authenticating reports of Marian sightings. (The sites listed above have been validated as authentic.) Beginning in 1981, at Medjugorje in the former Yugoslavia, reports of apparitions were published, and many Catholics traveled and found solace there. However, no official decision has yet been made about the nature of the Medjogorje events. While the Church presently does permit personal travel to Yugoslavia, church-sponsored groups such as parishes have not been permitted to organize pilgrimages to any sites that have not been formally authenticated.

Not all pilgrimages are undertaken to sites of apparitions. In fact, most are to other holy places or to shrines built to memorialize or honor an event or a holy person. Several pilgrimage sites in the United States today attract intense attention. For example, the Shrine of Our Lady of Charity in Florida is a magnet for the exiled Cuban Catholic community. The Basilica of the Immaculate Conception in Washington, D.C., the National Shrine of Our Lady of the Snows in Illinois, and The Cross in the Woods National Shrine in Indian River, Michigan, which includes the Shrine of Blessed Kateri Tekakwitha, are among the many examples of North American shine sites that attract Catholic pilgrims each year.

Pilgrimages are always interior as well as exterior journeys. The pilgrimage destination is not merely geographical; it is psychological and spiritual. The physical sacrifices, such as walking long distances, enduring pain, staying in inhospitable accommodations, or tolerating strange companions, have their interior analogues. One's rough edges are being worn away, one is being purged of one's reliance on creature comforts, and one learns to rely on God. The physical arrival at a holy place is as much about the recognition of a changed self as about seeing the fabled spot. But often at the time of arrival, encounters or realizations do take place in a heart readied by the arduous journey.

The shear physicality of pilgrimage—its embodiment—is significant. Spiritual transformation may come about through the body as well as through more mental disciplines. As with any sort of religious practice, openness to God's indwelling is a prerequisite, but the very acting out of the process, for example by enduring the rigors of a pilgrimage, may facilitate personal change. Often pilgrims take upon themselves some special sacrifice: walking on their knees the last miles to a shrine or fasting during their transit. This instinct to sacrificial offering of self is sometimes undertaken in gratitude for the redemptive sufferings of Christ, but it also prepares the person for a change. It clears out, strips away, cleanses, and allows for the letting go necessary to any true conversion of life.

LABYRINTH WALKING

Walking the labyrinth is at present a popular modern American variant of the traditional pilgrimage. Countless retreat centers and places of sacred rest around the country have installed these walking meditation paths using various mediums such as stone, earth, grass, concrete, canvas, or gravel. The practice emerged in Christian circles during the medieval era. When a pilgrimage journey to the Holy Land was not possible, perhaps because of distance, expense, or political upheaval, people could still walk a sacred pilgrim path—a labyrinth—marked out for them on the floor of a sacred place nearer home. Perhaps the most famous medieval labyrinth is in Chartres Cathedral just outside of Paris, a beloved sacred site dedicated to the Virgin and famous today for its glorious stained glass windows. On the central floor of the nave one finds an eleven-circuit pavement maze with a rosette design (associated with the Virgin) at its center. Sometimes this eleven-circuit labyrinth served as a substitute for an actual pilgrimage to Jerusalem, and as a result, it came to be called the Chemin de Jerusalem or "Road of Jerusalem." Alternately, the labyrinth could be walked as a penance. If so, it might be walked on one's knees. The labyrinth walker today, whether at Chartres or some other site, prepares as if embarking on an actual journey, and travels through each of four quadrants until he or she arrives at the center space of the labyrinth. It is typical for the prayer to make an intention before entering, or to carry with him or her a question, or simply to allow the slow, deliberate walk itself to unfold and speak its own truth. In the United States, some of the penitential aspect of the walking seems to have disappeared, but the excitement and mystery of the spiritual quest is still central to this embodied prayer.

DEVOTIONAL PRACTICES

Some of the most identifiable Catholic spiritual practices are ones that are often left out of descriptions of spirituality. These are devotional practices like veneration of the Sacred Heart or novenas to Our Lady of Perpetual Help or the wearing of the scapular of Our Lady of Mount Carmel. We have mentioned the popularity of Marian pilgrimages, but these are, of course, not the only Catholic practices associated with the Virgin Mary. There are literally thousands of devotions associated with the Blessed Virgin under her many titles. At the National Shrine of the Immaculate Conception in Washington D.C., dozens of altars are dedicated to the Blessed Virgin. Some represent titles of Mary that are held in special regard by religious congregations instrumental in the growth of the Church in the United States. For example, the Chapel of Mary Help of Christians in the upper church was donated by the Salesians of Don Bosco and the Daughters of Mary Help of Christians, international congregations founded in mid-nineteenth century Piedmont to minister to street children and at-risk youth. The religious and laity associated with the Salesian family were and still are ministering to the needs of America's most vulnerable young people. Similarly, the Dominicans sponsor the Chapel of Our Lady of the Rosary; the order's founder, Saint Dominic, is associated with the origins of rosary. In other chapels at the National Shrine, images of Our Lady of Siluva, Mary Queen of Ireland, and Our Lady of Czestochowa represent the Lithuanian, Irish, and Polish immigrants who are so important in the earlier history of the North American Church. These shrine chapels reveal Mary as patroness and intercessor, beloved by those groups who clothe themselves in her protective mantle.

This partial list, of course, represents only a fraction of the American shrines to Our Lady in her various guises. If these at the National Shrine tend to represent religious orders and immigrant communities that came to the United States earlier in its history, many others are sponsored and visited more recently by Catholics who came not from Europe, but from Latin and Central America, Asia, and Africa.

THE ROSARY

Among embodied devotional practices, there is also the most beloved and ubiquitous of Marian devotions, the rosary, practiced by millions of Catholics all over the world. The rosary is a wonderfully gestured prayer involving the fingering of beads and a meditative repetition of voiced prayers. The rosary, a circle of prayer beads divided into ten "decades" of beads, involves litany-like repetition of several classic prayers (the Lord's Prayer, Hail Mary, Apostles' Creed, and Glory Be to the Father) and silent meditation on the Joyful, Sorrowful, and Glorious Mysteries of the life of Mary and Jesus. The aim is, to use the words of twentieth century European theologian Romano Guardini, "participation in the life of Mary, whose focus was Christ."

The full spectrum of Mary's human experience and the cosmic implications of her role in salvation history are recapitulated in the rosary. We are, with her, joyful at the angel's greeting when she is told she will bear a son; when she hurries to tell her elderly cousin Elizabeth and sings a hymn magnifying God's name; when she brings her child into the world and presents him as a thank offering in the Temple; and when she finds him as a boy of twelve, teaching the teachers in Jerusalem. The Sorrowful Mysteries find us with Jesus and with his mother, who holds him in her heart, in the garden filled with foreboding about his upcoming death; at his scourging after his arrest; when he bears the cruel weight of a crown of thorns; while carrying the cross; and at his crucifixion and death. Finally, we and Mary are ushered into the mysteries that speak of glory: Jesus rises triumphant over death; he ascends to heaven after revealing himself to his grieving followers; those followers gather in the Upper Room where the promised Comforter descends and inspirits them; Mary, at her death, is assumed into heaven to be with her Son in anticipation of the joyful reunion for which we all hope; and after receiving from her Son the crown, Mary takes her place at his side as Queen of Heaven.

Traditionally these mysteries has been associated with a virtue exemplified in each of these scriptural moments: for example, humility, charity, detachment, obedience, patience, contrition, or conversion of heart. In addition, Pope John Paul II added to the rosary a set of Luminous Mysteries upon which to reflect. These focus on the life and ministry of Jesus, his baptism by John the Baptist in the river Jordan, his first miracle at the Wedding of Cana, his inaugural proclamation of the kingdom, his mountaintop transfiguration in the presence of several disciples, and his institution of the Eucharist during his final supper with his followers and friends.

Sometimes the rosary is prayed in a penitential manner: Mary is invoked as one whose intimacy with the Divine might carry our anguished prayers for a peaceful and renewed world to the One who is source and end of all. But even as she acts as intercessor, she also remains a model, the image of the new creation, the image of human beings made whole. The rosary is one of those delightfully embodied forms of prayer, a way of accessing the divine presence through the tactile fingering of beads, through the sound of rhythmic repetition, and, when prayed communally, by the patterning of imagination and memory through the antiphonal chant of leader and congregational response.

Not all devotions that utilize prayer beads are necessarily Marian in orientation or associated with the rosary. For example, a chaplet is a prayer form that uses fewer beads and has a specific devotional focus. The Chaplet of Blessed Kateri Tekakwitha is composed of eight brown, eight red, and eight crystal beads. The Chaplet of the Sacred Heart consists of thirty-three small beads, six large beads, a centerpiece, a crucifix, and a Sacred Heart medal. The love of God, played out in the short, faith-filled life of the "Lily of the Mohawks," and the infinite graciousness of divine love manifest in the Sacred Heart of Jesus are the focus of these chaplets. The Chaplet of the Seven Sorrows or Dolours, with its seven groups of seven beads, venerates the Virgin Mary under her aspects as the sorrowing mother whose heart is allied to that of her suffering child. The Chaplet of Our Lady, Star of the Sea, consists of a medal of Our Lady of Mount Carmel, plus three separate beads and twelve additional beads, and focuses on Mary as the guiding star by which we may safely navigate to the fullness of life, just as a mariner looks to the North Star for orientation on the tumultuous sea.

PROCESSIONS, FESTIVALS, AND SACRED THEATRE

In Boston's north end, that very traditional Italian Catholic neighborhood, community members hold colorful festivals in honor of the patron saints of Italy's various regions. They proceeed through the streets carrying statues of Saint Anthony of Padua and Santa Lucia, followed by marching bands and decorated floats. The surrounding neighborhood is trans- formed into a neighborhood celebration: food, music, and excited crowds fill the streets. In the Pilsen neighborhood of Chicago, an elaborate outdoor Living Way of the Cross (*Via Crucis*) is performed each year on Good Friday. Predominantly Mexicano, the Catholic community in this neighborhood has been staging this pageant since the late 1970s. City streets are blocked off, and costumed participants recite prayers at sites identified as symbolic of places of social injustice, violence, struggle, or solidarity. The Way culminates at a hill in Harrison Park, where three moreno men are raised on crosses and "crucified" before a weeping crowd. Whether observed as celebrations of ethnic and cultural identity or as embodied acts of solidarity and empowerment of an oppressed people, these sorts of religious processions, festivals, and sacred theatre are deeply embedded in the Catholic imagination.

From its medieval legacy, Catholicism gained its sense of the spiritual importance of embodied communal practices which encourage people to enact the truths of faith. While during the early modern reformation the Church did monitor some of the more flamboyant aspects of medieval festivals and celebrations, it nevertheless understood the importance of such rituals. The Jesuit Order especially, as it set out to evangelize the new world, relied on the power of elaborate public ritual and sacred theatre to affect and persuade hearts. The same was true of other great Church leaders during the nineteenth century. Saint Don Bosco is a case in point. Working with urban street boys, he created what he called a Festive Oratory which, along with religious instruction and vocational training, sponsored religious plays, games, and festivals. All of this was designed to win hearts and minds for the love of God. When the rough and brutalized children first came to him, Don Bosco took them for trips into the country and taught them games. They thus became part of a caring family. Yoking gentle, respectful education, advocacy, devotional practices, and popular piety, together with intellectual and vocational training in a spirit of joyful play, Bosco was remarkably effective in his ministries. The festival and the pageant were central to what he did for these forms of religious theatre; he both instructed his charges and drew them body and soul into the mysteries and the feasts they celebrated.

The formative capacity of religious theatre is still recognized across the Catholic world. May crownings in honor of the Virgin and Christmas pageants are still a part of many parochial school traditions. And the Filipino faithful in the United States bring with them from their home country the *Salubong*, an Easter dawn reenactment of the meeting of the sorrowful Mother and her newly risen Son. A procession of women carries the black-mantled statue of the Virgin, while a line of men bear the statue of the triumphant Christ aloft. Choirs of children dressed as angels sing out joyously as the two meet, the Virgin's black head covering is replaced with a white veil, and the great mystery of the resurrection is brought to light once again. At Christmas time the *posada*, the beloved Christmas custom of Mexican-American Catholics, takes place. The ritual involves a nine-day celebration, beginning December sixteenth and ending December twenty-fourth, which symbolizes the trials that Mary and Joseph endured before finding a place to stay where Jesus could be born. A particularly colorful *las posadas* is enacted each year on historic Olvera Street in central Los Angeles. Each night, the faithful bear a statue of the holy couple, sing and carry candles, and proceed door to door before they are finally welcomed inside on the final night of the celebration.

Festivals abound on December twelfth, the feast of Our

Lady of Guadalupe, patroness of the Americas. Her festival is celebrated throughout the United States with great joy. Often her day begins with *Las Mañanitas*, the tradition of gathering before dawn on the steps of the church to wake her. Musicians lead the gathered devotees in singing lilting songs that honor her beauty and the love that she engenders. The well-known story of Guadalupe's encounter with the indigenous peasant Juan Diego is often reenacted at the Mass that follows. Parishioners may dress the part of the beautiful lady in Christianized garb of an Aztec princess; of the startled Juan Diego, charged with conveying the Lady's message that she would like a sanctuary built in her honor; and of the Franciscan bishop he tries to convince of the authenticity of the encounter. As the legend affirms, the Lady did produce the evidence the bishop required: a shower of roses of Castile, plucked from a barren winter hillside, and a replica of her own appearance astonishingly captured on the cloak the peasant wore. December twelfth is the day when many Catholic churches throughout the country are filled with the scent and color of hundreds or thousands of roses, brought by the devout to honor and entreat *la Virgen Moreno*. Churches may offer a novena or a three-day preparation leading up to the feast. Processions with banners honoring Guadalupe are frequent.

Festivals and processions are part of the vocabulary of Catholic life. Whether they are part of the official liturgical life of parishes or organized by the faithful as expressions of devotion to a particular Madonna, a native saint, or a significant feast day, these embodied practices have a life and energy that shapes lives.

NOVENAS

Not all devotional practices involve festivals and religious theatre. Some involve time-specific gatherings that fall outside of the liturgical celebration and may be orchestrated by laity, as well as by clergy. As we have observed, Mary is venerated in the Catholic tradition under a thousand titles. One universally popular title is Our Lady of Perpetual Help, who is frequently invoked in a novena. A novena is a traditional practice of prayer, done either privately or communally on a pattern of nine days or nine weeks, which focuses on obtaining special graces. The Novena to Perpetual Help is particularly popular among Filipino Catholics. It was the Redemptorist Order that, in the nineteenth century, first promoted the Byzantine-style image of Mary as Perpetual Help. The power of the image to effect conversion of life was legendary. The Redemptorists took Perpetual Help with them to all their mission fields. In the Philippine Islands, the devotion was enthusiastically embraced and then was brought to the United States with immigration. Wednesday night is for this community the time when crowds of the faithful gather for Mass and a novena to Our Lady of Perpetual Help. There she is invoked as maternal refuge and comfort in time of trial, her maternal listening ear and empathic heart always open to those who entreat her aid.

Novena prayer can be variously enacted and variously directed. There is the Advent *Simbang Gabi* ("Dawn Mass") tradition observed by the Filipino Catholic community. For each of nine days before Christmas, a novena of Masses dedicated to the Virgin is celebrated as early as four in the morning. Parish churches are full, the music is festive, the preaching, sometimes by a visiting preacher, is stirring. The faithful rise early and make their way to the churches for this period as a way of preparing spiritually for the great mystery of the Nativity.

A newly popular novena observed throughout the United States and directed toward Jesus is the Divine Mercy Novena. It begins on Good Friday and culminates on the Saturday after Easter. The devotion was inaugurated in the early twentieth century as the result of the visions of a Polish nun, Sister Faustina, and has the express purpose of interceding for the spiritual succor of the entire world. On each day of the novena, the devotee brings to the merciful God (represented by a distinctive image of Jesus, his arms outstretched with rays of light emanating from his heart), a different group of persons and prays that they will be immersed in the ocean of divine mercy.

The deep ritual wisdom of the novena lies in its ability to create and cement community, and in its capacity to direct deep emotions born of the burden of living and transform them into hope. Gathering in a shared space and time for a common, self-transcending purpose bonds participants.

FIRST FRIDAYS AND FIRST SATURDAYS

Since earliest times, the community that followed the Way wanted to intimately grasp the mystery of divine graciousness that loved to the death for humankind. The Body of Christ, with its opened wounds and pierced side and heart, has long been the focus of devotion. Prompted by the visions of late seventeenth century Visitation sister, Margaret Mary Alacoque, the Church instituted a series of devotional practices that adored the Sacred Heart, the source of that magnanimous love. An annual feast, celebrated in the days following the eucharistic feast of Corpus Christi; a Thursday night adoration followed by a first Friday of the month observance; these were the devotions that honored the Sacred Heart of Jesus. While first Fridays may be less universally observed today than they were before the Second Vatican Council (which emphasized the Sunday eucharistic feast), they are nonetheless part of the Catholic landscape.

Saturdays are also days of special observance for some Catholics. Vietnamese American Catholics, heavily concentrated as a community in Orange County, California, are deeply devoted to Mary in her aspect as Our Lady of Fatima. As such, they enthusiastically have embraced the practice of gathering on Saturday for Mass, confession, and recitation of the rosary as prescribed in the 1917 Marian apparitions in Fatima, Portugal. According to those who are thus devoted, Mary's request to the children to whom she appeared was that they should gather for five first Saturdays in order to obtain her blessing. These time-specific devotions have the capacity to enable persons who observe them to remain attentive to the presence of God in their lives and in the world, and to encourage the flowering of faith, hope, and love. In common with other devotional practices, indeed even participating in the Eucharist if attendance is viewed as merely fulfilling an obligation, time-specific devotions may also serve "magical" rather than spiritually life-giving purposes. But they do not necessarily do so. They may be the vehicles through which God works to encourage spiritual maturation and transformation.

SACRAMENTALS

Whatever form they take, sacramentals are part of the Catholic embodied sensibility. Certain acts such as blessing, genuflecting, and making the sign of the cross are examples of sacramentals. Other familiar sacramentals are medals, scapulars, candles, or water blessed by a priest. The medal remains an important "sacramental" that Catholics may use to enhance a sense of the intimacy with the Divine.

In Perryville, Missouri, at the Shrine of Our Lady of the Miraculous Medal, a thriving center of Marian devotion has grown up under the auspices of the Vincentians. The origins of the devotion to the Miraculous Medal are in Paris, where in 1830, Catherine Labouré, a novice in the Daughters of Charity, experienced several apparitions in which the Virgin entrusted her with the mission of designing a medal. If worn, the medal would bring graces such as patience, forgiveness, repentance, and faith to the wearer. Today, devotees from all over the world send their petitions to the Perryville shrine, and votive candles are lit there for each of their prayers. There are so many requests that, to insure fire safety, the votive candles are now electric.

The Brown Scapular of Our Lady of Mount Carmel is another traditional Catholic sacramental. According to medieval legend, Mary appeared to Carmelite friar Saint Simon Stock and promised protection and intercessory aid to those who wear the scapular, a small version of her garment. The various branches of the Carmelites have, over the years, sponsored confraternities and secular institutes for lay persons who wish to live a more committed life in the Carmelite spirit. Formation may involve participation in the Liturgy of the Hours, meditation, or study of the writings of the Carmelite saints like Teresa of Ávila and John of the Cross. Wearing of the Brown Scapular is one part of the identity for many of those thus initiated.

Sacramentals can be misused if viewed as magical formulas or amulets, but on a deeper level, like visual images and visual prayer, they remind us that God's Spirit works precisely through the material world and the invisible is made visible. Our touch, taste, sight, hearing, smell, gestures, postures, and movements can be directed toward bringing us into a more vivid awareness of the divine milieu in which we live and move and have our being. It is no accident that the popular Catholic prayer of Saint Patrick not only places the one who prays in the beauty and majesty of creation and images God in embodied form, but that it also experiences God's protective presence on the crown of creation, the human body:

> I arise today
> through the strength of heaven,
> light of the sun,
> radiance of the moon,
> splendor of fire,
> speed of lightning,

swiftness of the wind,
depth of the sea,
stability of the earth,
firmness of the rock.
I arise today
through Gods' strength to pilot me,
God's might to uphold me,
God's wisdom to guide me,
Gods' eye to look after me,
God's ear to hear me,
God's word to speak to me,
God's hand to guard me,
God's way to lie before me,
God's shield to protect me,
God's hosts to save me
from the snares of the devil,
from everyone who desires me ill,
afar and near, alone or in a multitude,
Christ with me, Christ before me, Christ behind me,
Christ in me, Christ beneath me, Christ above me,
Christ on my right, Christ on my left,
Christ when I lie down, Christ when I sit down,
Christ when I arise,
Christ in the heart of everyone who thinks of me,
Christ in the mouth of everyone who speaks of me,
Christ in the eye that sees me,
Christ in the ear that hears me.

Sources Cited

Alphonsus de Liguori: Selected Writings. Trans. Frederick M. Jones. Classics of Western Spirituality Series. Mahwah, NJ: Paulist Press, 1999.

Angela of Foligno: Complete Works. Trans. Paul Lachance, OFM. Classics of Western Spirituality Series. Mahwah: NJ, Paulist Press, 1993.

Berken, Kathy. *Walking on a Rolling Deck: Life on the Ark.* Liturgical Press, 2008.

The Catechetical Instructions of St. Thomas Aquinas. Trans. Rev. Joseph B. Collins.

Chase, Steven. *Tree of Life: Models of Christian Prayer.* Baker, 2005.

Day, Dorothy. *Loaves and Fishes.* Harper and Row, 1963.

Desert Wisdom: Sayings from the Desert Fathers. Intro. Henri J. M. Nouwen. Maryknoll, NY: Orbis, 2001.

Hauser, Richard J. *Finding God in Troubled Times.* Chicago: Loyola University Press, 2002.

Ignatius of Loyola: Spiritual Exercises and Selected Works. Ed. George Ganss, SJ. Classics of Western Spirituality Series. Mahwah, NJ: Paulist Press, 1991.

Linn, Dennis, Sheila Fabricant Linn, Matthew Linn. *Sleeping with Bread: Holding What Gives You Life.* Mahwah, NJ: Paulist Press, 1995.

McGinn, Bernard. *The Foundations of Mysticism.* Vol. 1. New York: Crossroads, 1991.

Merton, Thomas. *New Seeds of Contemplation.* New York: New Directions Press, 1962.

———. *The Hidden Ground of Love: Letters of Thomas Merton on Religious Experience and Social Concerns*. Ed. William H. Shannon. New York: Farrar, Straus, Giroux, 1985.

Nouwen, Henri J.M. *The Return of the Prodigal Son: A Story of Homecoming*. New York: Doubleday Image Books, 1994.

———. *Behold the Beauty of the Lord: Praying with Icons*. Ave Maria Press, 2007.

———. *Praying with Ignatius Loyola*. Word Among Us Press, 2004.

Rolheiser, Ronald. *The Holy Longing*. New York: Doubleday Image Books, 1999.

St. Francis de Sales: Introduction to the Devout Life. Trans. John K. Ryan. New York: Doubleday, 1966.

St Thérèse of Lisieux: Essential Writings. Ed. Mary Frohlich. New York: Orbis Books, 2003.

Sister Thea Bowman: Shooting Star: Selected Writing and Speeches. Ed. Celestine Cepress. LaCrosse, WI: Franciscan Sisters of Perpetual Adoration, 1999.

Wiederkehr, Macrina. *Seasons of Your Heart: Prayers and Reflections*. San Francisco: Harper, 1979.

Wright, Wendy M. *Sacred Heart: Gateway to God*. New York: Orbis Books, 2001.

Further Reading: Classic and Contemporary

Bergan, Jacqueline Syrup and Marie Schwan. Take and Receive Series. Includes Book 1: *Love: A Guide to Prayer*; Book 2: *Forgiveness: a Guide to Prayer*; Book 3: *Birth: a Guide to Prayer*; Book 4: *Surrender: a Guide to Prayer*; Book 5: *Freedom: a Guide to Prayer;*. Saint Mary's Press, 1988.

Brading, D.A. *Mexican Phoenix: Our Lady of Guadalupe, Image and Tradition Across Five Centuries.* Cambridge University Press, 2003.

Carretto, Carlo. *Letters from the Desert.* Maryknoll, NY: Orbis, 2002.

Casey, Michael. *Sacred Reading: the Ancient Art of Lectio Divina.* Liguori Publications, 1996.

Day, Dorothy. *The Long Loneliness.* Harper One, 1996.

Elizondo, Virgil. *Guadalupe: Mother of the New Creation.* Orbis Books, 1997.

Griffin, Emilie. *Simple Ways to Pray: Spiritual Life in the Catholic Tradition.* Rowman and Littlefield Publishers, 2005.

Hart, Thomas N. *The Art of Christian Listening.* Mahwah, NJ: Paulist Press, 1980.

Keating, Thomas. *Intimacy with God: an Introduction to Centering Prayer.* Crossroad Publications, 1996.

Liebert, Elizabeth. *The Way of Discernment: Spiritual Practices for Decision Making.* Westminster John Knox, 2008.

Spiritual Directors International, www.sdiworld.org/.

Vanier, Jean. *Community and Growth: Our Pilgrimage Together.* Mahwah, NJ: Paulist Press, 1989.

Note: There are many translations of the classic texts in the Catholic spiritual tradition suggested below and throughout this handbook. Some noteworthy series of translations that can be recommended are the Paulist Press Classics of Western Spirituality series, which has many of the texts cited published under the author's name; the Institute of Carmelite Studies series on Carmelite authors; the Cistercian Publications translations of Cistercian Fathers; and the Modern Spiritual Masters series, published in the United States by Orbis Books.

Aelred of Rievaulx, *On Spiritual Friendship*
Brother Lawrence of the Resurrection,
    Practice of the Presence of God
Francis de Sales, *Introduction to the Devout Life*
John of the Cross, *Ascent of Mount Carmel* and
    Dark Night of the Soul
Pierre de Caussade, *Abandonment to Divine Providence*
Teresa of Ávila, *Interior Castle*
Thérèse of Lisieux, *Story of a Soul*

Charisms in the Body of Christ

There are different kinds of spiritual gifts but the same Spirit; there are different forms of service but the same Lord; there are different workings but the same God who produces all of them in everyone. To each individual the manifestation of the Spirit is given for some benefit. To one is given through the Spirit the expression of wisdom; to another the expression of knowledge according to the same Spirit; to another faith by the same Spirit; to another gifts of healing by the one Spirit; to another mighty deeds; to another prophecy; to another discernment of spirits; to another variety of tongues; to another interpretation of tongues. But one and the same Spirit produces all of these, distributing them individually to each person as he wishes.

1 Corinthians 12:4–11

1. Offices/Gifts

When Saint Paul spoke of the Mystical Body of Christ, he spoke of the gifts of the Spirit given to certain people. Not for their own edification, but for the health and flourishing of the entire body. In one of his letters to the church at Corinth (1 Corinthians 12), the apostle enumerated some of the varieties of spiritual gifts: knowledge, faith, healing, prophecy, discernment of spirits, and the gifts of speaking in and interpreting tongues. To the Ephesian church (chapter 4), Paul spoke plainly of the harmonious interplay between all the members of the body, some who are gifted with the spirit to be apostles, prophets, evangelists, pastors, and teachers. These gifts, or charisms as they are often called, are not best perceived as simply roles that are assigned or rigid categories into which members of the body are fitted. Rather, the idea of charisms suggests that the Christian community is a dynamic, Spirit-energized whole in which each particular person in his or her uniqueness is called and inspired by God to participate.

The Dogmatic Constitution on the Church (*Lumen Gentium*), which emerged from the Second Vatican Council, speaks of charisms in the following way. "[The Spirit] distributes special graces among the faithful of every rank. By these gifts, he makes them fit and ready to undertake the various tasks and offices for the renewal and building up of the church..." (*LG* 12). Reflection on this has led some scholars to consider what charisms the larger world of the twenty-first century might look like and to explore the gifts as they might emerge and energize the preacher, the biblical exegete, the parent, the new evangelizer, and the voiceless. "Where need is, there is charism," they conclude, viewing charisms as gifts that "enable many people to do ordinary things extraordinarily well" in order to build up families, neighborhoods, and cities, as well as the ecclesial body (*Retrieving Charisms for the Twenty-First Century*).

2. Traditions of Spirituality

The Christian spiritual life may be about "living Jesus," but there is no one way to do that. There is no generic holiness, no single path to perfection, no cookie-cutter model of the Christ-life. Instead, each person must discover, with the aid of the Scriptures, tradition, the witness of holy ones, and the guidance of others, what it means to "live Jesus" in the concrete specificity of his or her location, moment in history, talents, responsibilities, and sense of call.

At the same time, our Catholic spirituality involves a deep sense of a common life expressed in our relationship to the Mystical Body, our common prayer, the rhythm of the liturgical cycle, and in our communion with the cloud of witnesses. But our unity is never uniformity. In fact, the tradition in which we find ourselves is a rich and variegated one. If we look at it in terms of vocation, there is not one Catholic vocation, no one way of being married, no one way of being a religious or a priest, no one way of living the single life. Nor is there only one way of acting for the common good; we may do that as teachers, preachers, healers, business leaders, artists, volunteers, parents, friends, advocates, and so forth. The list is inexhaustible. Similarly, if we look at it historically, we can see that there are innumerable forms and varieties of ways that persons, individually and together, have responded to the promptings of God's enlivening Spirit. Yet there is commonality to all this diversity. In the seventeenth century, Saint Francis de Sales, who has also merited the title doctor of the Church, coined the term unidiverse, meaning unity in diversity. The term implies neither rigid uniformity nor individualistic anarchy. Rather, it suggests our deep identity in love in the Mystical Body of Christ.

That deep love that binds us and the fact that we share a story and common prayer means that the variety of ways in which we live out the Christ-life have a family resemblance: we are part of a long tradition. It is possible to trace that tradition through the centuries and to see how the many forms that Catholic spirituality has taken build on each other. Jesus is the paradigm. The kenotic pattern of his birth, life, death, and resurrection are the foundation upon which the entire tradition, and within that, many diverse traditions, are built. As the community that followed Jesus grew and developed, it found itself confronted with different political, cultural, and geographical circumstances. Each period and place called for a new response. In other words, the Spirit, inspiring a living tradition, breathed new breath into each generation. At the same time, the forms of Christian response, the lifestyles and forms of response of a particular era, do not disappear in the next period of time; they continue to enrich the Church.

MARTYRS

The Scriptures tell us that the very earliest followers of Jesus were often not received well by their contemporaries. The Acts of the Apostles narrates the way that Stephen, while "filled with grace and power" and "working great signs among the people," was stoned to death in Jerusalem; it also records the death of James, the brother of John, at the command of King Herod. Similarly, other early documents suggest that the martyrdoms of Peter and Paul, those great architects of the early faith, took place in Rome during the persecutions of the emperor, Nero. Nero was not alone among Roman emperors in distrusting the fledgling Christian community, which was not legally recognized as a legitimate religion, but often seen as an atheistic threat to the stability of the Empire and its gods. For the first three centuries, persecutions of Christians within the Empire created many martyrs who paid with their lives for witnessing to the truth of the Christ event. These heroic men and women were seen by their contemporaries as second Christs, and their deaths were envisioned as second baptisms that would usher them to the side of Christ in glory. The passion stories of the early martyrs were told and retold. Legendary was Ignatius, bishop of Antioch, condemned to death for his faith, who wrote letters to his flock from the ship where he was being transported to the Roman Coliseum to die. Ignatius spoke of himself as grain to be ground by the teeth of wild beasts so that he, like Christ, could become bread for the community. "Suffer me," he implored, "to be an imitator of the passion of my God." In similar fashion, the elderly Polycarp, burned in the amphitheater at Smyrna, was understood by the Christian community to be ritually re-enacting the passion and death of Jesus in his arrest and death. Two North African women, the noble-born Perpetua and the slave Felicity, were remembered for the stirring way in which they met their deaths at Carthage, giving up their children and family ties for the crime of being baptized into the Christian faith. This unique account, the central chapter of which was written by Perpetua herself, recounts the dramatic events that occurred at the cusp of the third century in North Africa. Among the startling insights gained through the narrative is the extent to which these early Christians experienced themselves as living at the threshold of a new reality of such beauty and significance that they were willing to give all for it. Equally striking is the fact that the protagonists of the story, a young matron and a slave girl, are persons who in the Greco-Roman culture of the time were not the typical heroes. But in the transformed cosmos which Perpetua and Felicity believed was dawning, such conventions, along with familial and biological certainties, would be overturned. The dynamic work of the Spirit is evident throughout the martyrology: Perpetua is privileged with prophetic dreams and gifts of reconciliation and healing, and the women and their fellow catechumens meet physical death with the certainty that it is a second birth into a new, transfigured life.

The early martyrs have significance for the history of spirituality in that in a real sense, they provide the first examples of the classic pattern of the Christian spiritual life lived out in the community of faith: the death and resurrection of Jesus recapitulated quite literally. "If we live, we live for the Lord, and if we die we die for the Lord; so then, whether we live or die, we are the Lord's. For this is why Christ died and came to life, that he might be Lord of both the dead and the living," Paul wrote in his letter to the Romans (14:8–9). That the martyrs, like Christ, conquered death was assumed. It was believed that they entered immediately into their new, eternal life. In the words of historian Peter Brown, the first martyrs were seen to "leapfrog the grave." In fact, these holy ones, filled with the Spirit's power, were perceived as channels of divine power. Their remains and the objects associated with them in life continued to be conduits through which the persecuted community believed it could contact the divine. The tombs of the martyrs became gathering places for the faithful where their stories were retold. And in the same way that people flocked to the apostles like Stephen, who "worked signs and wonders" in the power of the Spirit, so many flocked to the martyrs' tombs, bringing their lame, blind, deaf, and infirm for healing. The Christ event, which for the early church inaugurated a new eon, was experienced as being ushered in the with the martyrs' sacrifice.

Martyrdom as a form of spiritual practice is not, of course, something that should be sought out. But social and political circumstances have continued to produce Christian martyrs over the centuries. Each era has produced its martyrs, but some eras and circumstances have provided occasions for the enactment of this ultimate witness. The early persecution of the emergent Church under several Roman emperors produced the most well-known martyrs. But later eras did as well. The Reformations of Europe sadly gave many occasions for inter-Christian conflict. Especially notable were the deaths of those Catholics who resisted the English Reformation and paid for their faith with their lives. These included, famously, Sir Thomas Moore, a humanist scholar and statesman who was hanged, and Cardinal John Fisher, who was beheaded, for refusing to acknowledge the legitimacy of King Henry VIII's claim to be the supreme head of the Church of England. Margaret Clitherow was crushed to death for illegally harboring priests in her home, and a number of Jesuits were martyred for entering the country in order to minister underground to the recusant population that was deprived of sacramental ministry under English law. Even more dramatically, the missionary expansion of Christianity across the globe, beginning at the end of the fifteenth century and continuing into the nineteenth, produced martyrs. French Jesuits including Issac Jogues, Jean de Brebeuf, Antoine Daniel and Jean de Leland, sent to evangelize the native populations in "New France" (French Canada) in the seventeenth century, were tortured and martyred during the fierce wars between the Hurons and the Iroquois. That same century saw the persecution of the nascent Catholic Church in Japan, during which those who refused to abandon their faith were executed. Vietnam too had its martyrs in the seventeenth, eighteenth, and nineteenth centuries, most notably Andrew Dung-Lac, martyred for the crime of being a priest. He is officially remembered along with one hundred and seventeen other Vietnamese Catholics of those centuries who witnessed to their faith with their lives. Korea had its martyrs in the nineteenth century;

thousands of ordinary Catholics suffered under a government that suppressed Christian observance, among whom priest Andrew Kim Taegon and lay catechist Paul Chong Hasang have been canonized. China was another Asian mission field that experienced governmental resistance to the continuation of Catholic missions that had been planted, especially during the nineteenth century Boxer Rebellion. The African Church has its martyrs, too. In the nineteenth century, Uganda King Mwanga of Buganda, threatened by the fact that converts put loyalty to their faith before loyalty to the king, burned African Catholics and Anglicans for their misguided commitments.

The twentieth century has the perhaps dubious distinction of being the century of Christian martyrs par excellence. Official recognition by the Church of some who died for the faith has occurred. Among them are hundreds of Spanish priests, bishops, deacons, monks, and nuns caught in the crossfire of the Spanish Civil War. Individuals from other regions include Blessed Miguel Pro of Mexico (1891-1927), the Venerable Charles de Foucauld of Algeria (1858-1916), Blessed Franz Jagerstatter of Austria (1907-43), Saint Edith Stein of Germany (1891-1942), and Saint Maximilian Kolbe of Poland (1894-1941), the last three of whom were victims of the Nazi regime. Stein, a philosopher, Carmelite nun, and convert from Judaism, is considered by the Church to be a martyr, condemned as a consequence of the Dutch hierarchy's 1942 public condemnation of Nazi racism. Stein had transferred to Carmel in the Netherlands when the decree was published, and Nazi retaliation resulted in the extermination of Catholic converts of Jewish background. Franciscan Kolbe was interred by the Third Reich for being an intellectual and a journalist, and canonized for his final act of taking the place of a fellow prisoner who had been sentenced to starve to death. Jaegerstatter was an Austrian peasant whose faith-filled conscience would not allow him to participate in Hitler's forced military duty. His heroic and solitary witness (fellow villagers considered him foolish or deluded) led to his death by guillotine.

The Church has long recognized and venerated those who gave their lives for the faith. As has been the case since the earliest era, there are people who have died and who are looked upon by the faithful as true martyrs (in other words, they were killed specifically for their faith, not for other reasons), but who are not listed on the official calendar of saints. The late twentieth century deaths in El Salvador of Archbishop Oscar Romero, four American women working among the poor with Maryknoll missions, and six Jesuit professors at the University of El Salvador, along with their housekeeper and her daughter, are memorialized by many in North America as martyrdoms. Hundreds of thousands of others in Europe, Latin America, and Asia, named and un-named, both individuals and groups, can be listed alongside the universally acknowledged few who died over the centuries for their heroic witness, their literal participation in the ongoing life of Christ.

DESERT TRADITIONS AND ASCETIC MARTYRDOM

Heroic witness in the form of blood martyrdom, while it is paradigmatic, is not the way most Christians have been actually called to live the spiritual life. Yet the kenotic dynamic of death and resurrection remains a foundational pattern. As the Christian community became legal and then became the sole religion of the late Roman Empire in the fourth century, a new movement arose. Serious disciples, critical of the way in which church affiliation was taken lightly and discipleship was watered down, went out into the Egyptian, Palestinian, and Syrian deserts to "die to self" and live in Christ. The values that shaped late antique civil society—pride, self-aggrandizement, luxury, and greed—were contrasted with values that Christ was seen to embody: humility, simplicity, singleness of heart, compassion, and constant prayer. The desert was believed to be a formative environment in which the "false self" created by society could be deconstructed and the "true self" could come to life. Saint Anthony of Egypt (c. 251–356) was the archetypal holy person born of the desert's rigors. Attending church in his town, Anthony heard a sermon preached on the twentieth chapter of the Gospel of Mark in which Jesus invites a man seeking a perfect life to "sell all you have, give your money to the poor, and follow me." Anthony took the invitation personally and seriously. His parents had passed away, so he sold all his possessions, made arrangements for an unmarried sister to be cared for, and put himself under the instruction of a local spiritual guide. As he prayed, Anthony began to discern a call to an ascetic lifestyle, one dedicated to overcoming the body's inordinate demands in order to free the spirit. He lived alone, wove baskets, fasted, slept little, conversed sparingly, prayed continuously, and owned nothing but the bare necessities.

The discipline he underwent was not primarily physical, however. Even as he withdrew from the formative environment of the city, Anthony discovered that those inner qualities that society honors were not easily overcome: they were lodged deep in the human heart. The interior struggle began. He sought to die to self in order to be reborn in Christ. Anthony and his contemporaries described this interior struggle with the language of spiritual warfare. During his long life, this most notable desert ascetic moved farther and farther away from the center of civilization. Yet his fame as a self-authenticating holy man constantly increased, and disciples followed him out to the remote regions where he dwelt. Most notably, he was visited by Athanasius, bishop of Alexandria, who recorded his life in a widely circulated book.

Anthony is known as the father of desert asceticism, but he was only one of many Christians who were drawn to the transformative silence and solitude of the deserts. The self-emptying pattern of their lives, which made space for divine presence, was to become the template for centuries of spiritual seekers. Disciples came to sit at the feet of the holy men and women, the abbas and ammas (fathers and mothers) of the desert. The neophytes would ask for a "word" from a spiritual mentor, a word discerned by the master and fitted to unlock the particular spiritual door that a disciple needed to open. These words, recorded and collected later as Sayings of the Desert Fathers, stand as testimony to the spare, insightful wisdom that the desert dwellers imparted.

They propose a vision of spiritual maturity that remains relevant today: a person of self-discipline, deep compassion, humility, and responsiveness to the Spirit of God, all ripened in silence and solitude. The solitary life, while certainly not the life of most Catholics through the centuries, has nonetheless remained an enduring part of the spiritual tradition. It has taken various classic forms over the centuries: hermits, who lived alone and pursued prayer and ascetic practice, have been part of the landscape since the desert dwellers first explored this way of living the Christ life. There have also been hermit communities. In the early centuries, solitaries sometimes grouped themselves around a holy man, meeting individually with him for counsel and with one another for shared prayer. The eleventh century in Europe saw a vibrant revival of the eremitic (hermit) life. Two notable orders of hermits were founded: the Italian Camaldolese and the French Carthusians. Saints Bruno and Romuald led the way in this revival of interest in the life transformed in silence and solitude. Establishing houses far from the bustle of urban and commercial activity was paramount. La Grand Chartreuse, the mother house of the Carthusians, is high in the mountainous alps in an area that two centuries ago was deemed "desolate" by intrepid travelers. The monks there enjoy an uncompromising silence in which to pursue their chores and inner contemplation, a silence broken only by liturgical song, occasional business transactions, and the conversation that takes place during designated times of recreation.

Another variant of the eremitic life had a number of adherents in the fourteenth century. An anchorite or anchoress was generally a spiritually mature person, usually a woman, who chose to live a solitary life in a cell attached to a monastery or church. There was a formal ecclesial ritual by which an anchoress, after assuring that she had a dowry or sufficient means to contribute to her support, would be formally enclosed in her anchorhold by the bishop and dedicate herself to a life of solitary pursuit of God. Often such persons, and the English anchoress Julian of Norwich is a notable example, were sought out by others as guides, just like the desert ammas and abbas. We know from the accounts written by the lay woman and aspiring spiritual peritus Margery Kempe that for a short period during the day, Julian would come to the window of her anchorhold so that she could offer spiritual advice to those who sought her out.

A modern exemplar of the value of silence and solitude was American monk and popular spiritual writer Thomas Merton (1915–1968). A peripatetic childhood and wild youth preceded Merton's entry into an austere Trappist monastic community. While he was thus immersed in quiet, and at a distance from society's busy-ness due to the strict enclosure of his monastery in rural Kentucky, Merton felt called over the years to the even deeper silence and solitude of the eremitic life. He came to see the solitary individual ideally as the "marginal man," the one who has a unique and wise perspective on human experience. He especially felt that it is in silence and solitude that the hard work of peeling away the false self in order to live in Christ can be accomplished.

> ...the mission of the solitary [in today's world] is first the full recovery of man's human and natural measure. Not that the solitary merely recalls the rest of

men to an impossible Eden. But he reminds them of what is theirs to use if they can manage to extricate themselves from the web of myths and fixations which a highly artificial society has imposed on them. The hermit exists today to realize and experience in himself the ordinary values of a life lived with a minimum of artificiality....

The Christian solitary life today should bear witness to the fact that certain basic claims about solitude and peace are in fact true. And in doing this, it will restore people's confidence, first in their own humanity and beyond that in the grace of God.

CONTEMPLATION IN A WORLD OF ACTION

From his marginal vantage point, Merton wrote about contemplative prayer and inner transformation, but he also took a prophetic stance, writing with moral clarity about world issues like peace, racial tolerance, and social equality.

MONASTIC TRADITIONS

The ideals of the desert, the transformation of life in the image of Christ, certainly continue: there are still hermits and hermit orders. But they have taken on other forms as well. Even in the early deserts, it was discovered that the transformed life was best accomplished with help: wise advisors, principles to guide one, and a community to support the process of living into the disciplines of the Christian life. Leaders began to emerge who gave shape and structure to that life. Notable early founders of communities of monks (the word means "alone" or "single") in the eastern deserts were Basil, bishop of Caesarea (c. 330–379) and Pachomius (c. 292–348), who organized groups of ascetics under a common discipline with shared goods in order to regularize and facilitate the processes of individual transformation. Varieties of monastic orders grew up, each with its distinct regulations and customs, but they all shared the sense that they were the places that the Spirit did its work most visibly, places where conversion of life was nurtured. For over twelve centuries they provided the chief model of discipleship, an ascetic one, for the entire Christian world. Monasticism became one of the greatest and most influential of church institutions in the Roman Church. In terms of spirituality, members of monastic communities, male and female alike, developed the practices, provided the language, and gave literary expression to the processes of spiritual growth.

The monastic tradition with the most significance in the western Christian world was that founded by Saint Benedict of Nursia (c. 480–c. 547). The small Rule of Saint Benedict that provides the template for all Benedictine houses is a model of brevity and insight. In it, a monastery is described as being a "school for the service of the Lord." It speaks of the administration of the monastery (for example, how to order the day, choose leaders, lead effectively, provide for the group's needs) and of the spiritual development of community members. Incorporation into a Benedictine community is gradual; the person goes through a series of formative stages and finally takes vows to remain in this community for life. The three "evangelical councils" of poverty, chastity, and obedience are the basic guidelines for most vowed Catholic religious communities, but a Benedictine specifically promises stability, conversion of manners, and obedience. (Having no personal property and practicing celibacy are part of a monk's life and are assumed under the Benedictine vow of obedience.)

Benedictine life revolves around the rhythms of prayer and work (*Ora et Labora*). The brothers or sisters gather in common prayer for the Liturgy of the Hours throughout the day, and they spend time in private spiritual reading. This dedication to the "Work of God" (*Opus Dei* is the frequently used Latin term) is the core of their life, the sanctification of time at the heart of Benedictine spirituality. Work is the other important aspect. Most monasteries support themselves through some sort of common work. What is distinctive about monastic life is its shared character. When a person asks to be admitted to the monastery, he or she is queried, "What do you seek?" "The mercy of God and the fellowship of this community," is the appropriate answer. The common life of shared goods, shared prayer, shared meals, shared work, shared silence, hospitality, and shared observance of the Rule in pursuit of the transformed life: this is the Benedictine ideal.

The Benedictine monastic family has an illustrious history: its place in the preservation and creation of western culture is unquestioned. Western scholarship, education, sciences, literature, evangelization, theology, liturgy, music, art, architecture, crafts: these all have the Benedictine imprint in one way or another. Hence, its influence on the Catholic Church, that distinctive western form of Christianity, is likewise unparalleled. At the present, there are many different monasteries in the United States that belong to the Benedictine family. A sampling would include the monks of Saint John's Abbey in Collegeville, Minnesota, and the nearby Sisters of the Monastery of Saint Benedict, who are known primarily as the founders and educators of two distinguished Catholic colleges: the College of Saint Benedict and Saint John's University. Nestled in the Sangre de Cristo Mountains in New Mexico is the double monastery (one for men, one for women) of Our Lady of Guadalupe Abbey and the Olivetan Benedictine Sisters of Our Lady of Guadalupe Abbey. They form the Pecos Benedictine community and sponsor a center for retreats and Church renewal. The Benedictine monks of Weston Priory in Vermont are known for the church music they compose, which Catholics might recognize from parish songbooks. Saint Andrews Benedictine Abbey in central California markets the much-loved devotional ceramics created by Belgian Benedictine, Father Maur van Doorslaer. The Benedictine Sisters of Erie, Pennsylvania, in complementary contrast, have a strong justice orientation to their ministries. They are engaged in peacemaking initiatives, sponsoring retreats, and publishing material that nurtures the spirit for a more just world. All of these communities, whatever the particular work they engage in, have at their heart common prayer and a common rule designed to encourage ongoing conversion of life.

Those monastic communities that bear the name of Saint Benedict are not the only ones that follow his classic little Rule. As places that hold conversion of life in high regard, the monasteries and monastic communities have frequently generated reform movements. One of the most notable took place in the twelfth century, when a group of men, Bernard of Clairvaux the most illustrious of them, were critical of the way monastic life was being observed. They established the Cistercian Order, which sought to revitalize that life by more exactly following the original Rule of Saint Benedict. The early Cistercians established themselves in remote settings, far from the distractions of urban life. They placed an emphasis on the manual work that had been a hallmark of Benedict's own foundations and made simplicity of liturgy and architecture in order to not distract from the inner work of continual conversion. Cistercians underwent another reform in the seventeenth century, thus creating two branches: the Common Observance and the Strict Observance. Perhaps the most well-known American Cistercian is Thomas Merton, whose mid-twentieth century writings on topics ranging from the life of solitude, the monastic spirit, social issues like war, and interfaith encounter are classics. Contemporary Cistercian monastics, most notably Father Thomas Keating, are also originators of the popular Centering Prayer Movement, that modern adaptation of a traditional practice of contemplative prayer. And we owe to the Benedictine monastic traditions a debt of gratitude for the wisdom that can be attained through *lectio divina*, the scriptural prayer cultivated in such communities.

While Benedictine monasticism has been the most determinative in the history of the Church, it is not the only type of western monasticism. Notable is what has been called the

Celtic monastic tradition. Although the term Celtic is debated by historians, and it is generally agreed that what often is advertised as Celtic spirituality in America today has more to do with romantic notions than an actual past tradition, one can, in fact, use the term to refer to a type of Christian monastic spirit that flourished in Ireland, Wales, and Scotland, particularly in the medieval era. Unlike the Benedictine tradition, which was unified at least in its embrace of a single rule, Celtic monasticism was multiform. There are examples of lay abbots who passed down their offices to their sons (this was before clerical celibacy was normative). It could be very austere: the famous abbot Columbanus was intimidating in the uncompromising personal austerity he expected of himself and his monks. There was a strong tradition kinship and a tradition of female leadership. Saint Bridget of Kildare is still celebrated today. She was the founder of a double monastery of men and women and is fabled in legend as being able to make fields and human beings fertile. Many Irish monks were peripatetic; they wandered from place to place in imitation of Christ, who had no place to lay his head. The ancient saga, Voyage of Brendan, tells of the seafaring of the tenth century Irish saint, a tale replete with ancient Irish motifs, Christian apocalyptic visions, biblical reminiscences, early medieval zoological and geographical lore, and combined exact descriptions of monastic regime and ascetical ideals. From the Celtic monastic world we have inherited gorgeous traditions of manuscript illumination and religious poetry, both of which are sensitive to the natural world, the penitential system (which would develop into the practice of sacramental confession shared by the entire Church), insight into the nature of the Trinity, and an appreciation of the significance of the soul friend, or *anmchara*, in the spiritual life. Two Irish devotional poems, titled "The Lord of Creation" and "A Scribe in the Woods," may capture something of this unique tradition.

> Let us adore the Lord,
> Maker of marvelous works,
> Bright heaven with its angels,
> And on earth the white-waved sea.
>
> A hedge of trees surrounds me,
> a blackbird's lay sings to me,
> praise I shall not conceal,
> Above my lined book the trilling
> of the birds sings to me.
> A clear-voiced cuckoo sings to me in a gray cloak
> from the tops of
> bushes.
> May the Lord save me from Judgment;
> well do I write under
> the greenwood.

CELTIC SPIRITUALITY

MENDICANT TRADITIONS

The "evangelical counsels" of poverty, chastity, and obedience, observed by monastics for many centuries and given definitive western expression in the Benedictine way, defined the shape of the life that was conceived to be a perfect following of Christ. But in the late medieval era in the western Christian world, new social and ecclesial conditions arose that called for a new response. The result was the flourishing of the "mendicant" traditions. The term is given to those communities that originally relied on alms to survive. More specifically, it refers to new sorts of religious groups emerging in the thirteenth century that practiced a "mixed" life. The Franciscans, Dominicans, and Carmelites are the most well-known groups that have mendicant origins. Like the monks, the friars (or brothers as they sometimes referred to themselves) took prayer seriously, but they also believed that they were called to go out into the wider society and preach the Gospel.

Franciscans

The early Franciscans, for example, spent part of the year withdrawn from the hustle and bustle of the towns in order to more closely listen to what God had to say. Then they headed out to the streets to preach to the people. They were drawn to this way of life by their founder, Francis of Assisi. This most popular of Catholic saints has been described as someone who "performed the Gospel." Francis is remembered as a boisterous young man, son of an affluent cloth merchant in the burgeoning mercantile Italian town of Assisi. Francis' personal story of conversion took place against a wider backdrop of social and ecclesial change. There had been a diffuse growing movement of evangelical enthusiasm in western Christendom for some time. People were drawn to the ideals of the apostolic period and wanted to live the Gospel more seriously: they wanted to follow the model of Jesus and the early Christians who followed him. Francis himself was converted to this new way of life and gave it his own distinctive twist. His vision of the Christian life was inspired by two Gospel images, both that emphasized nakedness: God's love revealed, on the one hand, in a vulnerable naked infant in a manger, and, on the other hand, in the death of a naked, suffering cross-hung man. Francis' entire spirituality revolved around this theme and took the form of voluntary poverty as radical lifestyle and concern for the poor and outcast. Mostly, Francis preached the truth of the poverty of Christ with his actions. He is reputed to have enjoined his friends to "Preach the Gospel. If necessary, use words."

There were critiques implicit in Francis' performative practice. Through his poverty, he critiqued the affluent merchants of his day; through his radical egalitarianism, he critiqued the power and privilege of the hereditary aristocracy; by his peacemaking actions, he critiqued the Italian city states' culture of warfare; by his preaching to the birds and his poetic verses praising brother sun and sister moon, he honored God the Creator and critiqued contemporary theological movements that denied the goodness of the created world. Quickly, a band of committed followers gathered around the poor man of Assisi and joined him in his radical lifestyle in imitation of the poor Christ. Among those inspired by Francis was Clare of Assisi, a young noblewoman who was drawn by the same Spirit-led desire to witness to the radical love of God. Given the social conventions of the day, Clare and her band of like-minded females established an enclosed community which practiced poverty, not by begging in the streets or barter in kind, but by praying for the work of the friars. They existed on the alms of those whom they inspired.

The Franciscan movement was a popular one, and as the order grew, some of Francis' own radical stances were modified. For example, although the founder had great reverence for priests, he felt his band of poor men should not hold any sort of office, nor should they attain academic degrees. Yet in subsequent decades, Franciscan priests and scholars emerged. Among these were Saint Bonaventure (1221–1274) and Blessed Duns Scotus (1266–1308), both of whom have had enormous influence on Catholic theology. The former has been awarded the title, doctor of the Church, for the fulsomeness of his exposition on the faith. Among Bonaventure's many important philosophical, exegetical, and theological works, his *Life of Saint Francis: The Soul's Journey to God* and *The Tree of Life* hold pride of place for spirituality. While there were many beloved tales told of the Franciscan founder such as the *Fioretti* or "Little Flowers," Bonaventure's *Life* was meant to be the "official" story, which drew out from the tales the spiritual and moral vision of the poor man from Assisi who modeled Christ and thus presented a model for imitation. *The Souls' Journey* focuses rather on the mystical Christ and Christ the bridegroom, who is the gateway to contemplation and, ultimately, the darkness of mystical unknowing. *The Tree of Life* rounds out Bonaventure's Franciscan vision by focusing on the concrete historical details of the life and passion of

Jesus the man, although it is presented with a poetic, even rhapsodic prose. In this case, the focus of the meditation is upon Jesus as he is "dimmed in death":

> Then he who is "fairer in beauty than the sons of
> men" (Ps 44:3), with his eyes clouding and his cheeks
> turning pale, appeared ugly for the sons of men,
> having been made a holocaust with a most sweet
> fragrance in view of his Father's glory in order to
> "avert his anger" from us (Ps 84:4).
> O Lord, Holy Father, look down then,
> from your sanctuary
> from your lofty habitation in the heavens;
> look, I say, upon the face of your Anointed;
> look upon this most holy Victim
> which our High Priest offers to you
> for our sins
> and be placated over your people's wantonness.
> And you also, redeemed man, consider
> who he is, how great he is,
> and what kind of person he is
> who for you is hanging on the cross,
> whose death brings the dead to life,
> at whose passing away
> heaven and earth mourn and hard rocks crack
> as if out of natural compassion.
> O human heart,
> you are harder than any hardness of rocks,

> if at the recollection of such great expiation
> you are not struck with terror,
> nor moved with compassion
> nor shattered with compunction
> nor softened with devoted love.

THE TREE OF LIFE

The subsequent history of the Franciscan and Poor Clare movements are complex and varied. Suffice it to say that the many branches of the Franciscan family still hold to the spiritual values espoused by their founder while expressing these in different ways. Although their ministries are many and varied and they are found in dioceses all over the United States and the world, the Franciscan friars of the Santa Barbara Province in California will serve as an example of this contemporary continuity with the founder's vision. Their Web site explains:

> Together with the whole Franciscan family, we are challenged to adapt ourselves to a rapidly changing church and world while remaining true to the spirit of our founder, St. Francis. Like his original followers, Franciscans today are called to be persons of prayer involved in a variety of ministries. Our charism is not to any specific task in the Church. Rather, it is to be brothers among ourselves, to all people, and to all of God's creation.

WWW.SBFRANCISCANS.ORG/

To embody this mission, these men promote non-violent peacemaking, teach an ecological sensitivity toward the earth, and work for justice for the poor, especially immigrants. These are modern expressions of the Franciscan spirit.

Dominicans

Dominic Guzman was a Spanish contemporary of Francis and he too was moved by the new spirit coursing through the medieval church. His order, which, like the Franciscans, eventually included an enclosed women's branch and espoused the mixed life, was focused on preaching as well. However, as there have always been a variety of charisms in the church, Dominic and his disciples had their own way of responding to the Gospel imperative. Dominic, while a notable personality, has not attracted as much hagiographic attention as has the colorful saint from Assisi. Cheerful and energetic, Dominic was deeply moved by persons whom he perceived as lost sheep needing a shepherd. He lived a life of simple austerity, prayed simply, and desired that others be drawn into the truths of the Gospel. His first companions offered themselves to the papacy as itinerant preachers. This was an era deeply concerned about unorthodox versions of the faith, and the Dominicans led the campaign to teach the people well. Preaching the Word became central to the charism of the order. Preaching well required that those engaged in it be knowledgeable and so study was emphasized. Soon the Dominicans could be found in new universities of Paris and Oxford, debating the critical issues of the day, engaging with newly emerging philosophies and experimental sciences. Dominican spirituality honored the life of the mind and cultivated it as part of the journey to God. Saint Thomas Aquinas, whose influence in Catholic theology has been enormous since the thirteenth century, is an example of someone who embodied the Dominican search for truth, in his case, through intellectual inquiry into the mysteries of faith. Other notable members of the Dominican pantheon include a group known as the fourteenth century "Rhineland mystics." Meister Eckhart, John Tauler, and Henry Suso were part of a circle that preached compellingly in a specific mode that attracts interest in the contemporary world. Close to the heart of this German circle's message was the ancient teaching of negative or apophatic theology, which emphasized a movement toward the Divine into darkness or nothingness and the necessity for radical detachment. These Dominicans were very public preachers and enjoyed the admiration of many who came to hear them preach. They attended to the spiritual needs of lay penitents and the many religious women who shared their charism. Often, especially with Eckhart, their language was edgy, pushing the listener beyond familiar categories. As Meister Eckhart saw God as beyond human categories of comprehension, it followed that the approach to the Divine must be imageless. In a sermon on the Gospel of Luke, he strikes this note:

> "He had no name." Thus the unfathomable God is without names, for all the names that the soul gives him it takes from its own knowledge....I am not speaking of knowledge aided by grace, because

a person could be carried up by grace that he would understand as St. Paul did....God remains uncomprehended because he was caused by no one. He is always the first. He is also without a specific manner of being in his incomprehensibility. He is also without effects, that is, in his hidden stillness. This why he remains without names.

MEISTER ECKHART, TEACHER AND PREACHER

Eckhart's famous discussions of the Godhead beyond God into which the ardent follower must necessarily be drawn and of the birth of God in the soul, did not, however, suggest a withdrawl from active life. Quite the reverse, Eckhart and his compatriots were intensely engaged in public ministry. They, and later Dominicans, known as the Order of Preachers, made and continue to make that ministry central to their identity.

Third Orders and Lay Movements

Both the Franciscan and Dominican Orders grew up in an atmosphere of intense spiritual energy generated by ordinary Christian people. But not everyone could join the friars or enter a convent, and so these mendicant groups encouraged lay participation by sponsoring a variety of associate groups and founding Third (Tertiary) Orders. Men and women of spiritual mind who were householders, merchants, storekeepers and workers as well as titled landowners were inspired by the mendicant vision. They adopted modified rules of life under the tutelage of the mendicant friars which allowed them to live "in the world" with intentionality and guidance. Two such lay women would make their marks in the annals of holiness. Angela of Foligno, who lived a generation after the saint from Assisi, enjoyed a lavish and, by her own accounts, sensual existence until the deaths of her husband and sons. Embracing the Franciscan path, she affiliated herself with the tertiaries and dramatically altered her lifestyle. She went on pilgrimage to follow in Francis' footsteps, became noted as a charismatic spiritual leader, and gathered around herself a community of devoted disciples. In thoroughly Franciscan fashion, Angela identified with the "suffering God-man." Her book is a passionate account of her mystic encounters.

The Dominicans too count among their number a remarkable Third Order woman, Catherine of Siena, whose fierce love for the Church at a time of great ecclesial scandal caused her to preach to popes and princes alike. Her reputation for holiness and her gifts of interpreting the depths of the Catholic theological vision gained her not only a hearing by the powerful man of her day, but a devoted following who called her "mama" and looked to her as a seer and saint. Catherine's greatest writing, *The Dialogue*, is a marvel of rich insight into the redemptive love of God in Christ and the vital life of the Church, Christ's body.

Alongside these formally organized Third Orders, other loosely knit lay spiritual movements grew up in the late middle ages. Among these, the Beguines in the Low Countries of northern Europe are notable. The Beguines were a movement of lay women prompted to live intentional Christian lives. Prayer, charitable service, and spiritual formation were at the movement's heart. Some Beguines lived in their family homes, others lived in community. A few of the Beguinages, as they were called, were small villages where the women lived, prayed and worked. They were not ordered under canon law, however, and a woman might be part of a beguine community for a while and later leave to marry. The majority of the women (most were from the middle classes) supported themselves by handcrafts, weaving, and lace making. These beguine communities were not self-enclosed however, and many of the women participated in sacramental life in local parishes. The movement was fluid and eventually came to an end, but it produced some remarkable figures and spiritual literature. Marguerite Porete's *Mirror of Simple Souls*, Hadewijch of Brabant's poetry, and Mechtilde of Magdeburg's *Flowing Light of the Godhead* are among the treasures that come to us from this northern European women's movement.

In other parts of Europe, lay women were inspired by the *vita apostolica*. *Beatas* in Spain, female house ascetics in Italy, and the later Modern Devotion movement, which involved laity, religious, and clerics and which produced the famous devotional manual, *Imitation of Christ*, are all part of a larger history of lay spiritual movements in the Church in the late medieval period. Like the Third Orders, they represent a widening sense of what the Christ life entailed, a life no longer seen as necessarily involving a literal flight from the world.

Carmelites

The Carmelites are another order with mendicant origins that has played and continues to play an important role in Catholic life. The Carmelites trace their earliest beginnings to a group of hermits who were said to have taken up residence on Mount Carmel in the Holy Land in the twelfth century. Even more remotely, they see themselves as heirs to an eremitic tradition exemplified by the Old Testament Prophet Elijah, and it was near a rocky spring known as Elijah's fountain that these medieval hermits dwelt. Given a rule and "way of life" in the following century, they came to see themselves as living in allegiance to Jesus Christ though the alternating practices of solitude and preaching. From the desert tradition and from Elijah, the Carmelites inherited a love of solitude and a dedication to the interior struggle. But if the Prophet who was commanded by God to hide himself in a remote region where the ravens would feed him (1 Kings 17:2–4) is one model for Carmelites, Mary is the other. The tradition of Carmel likens her to the little cloud that Elijah saw: she is the rainwater arising from the salty sea, the pure human person who emerges from the salty brine of a sinful world. Mary is for them patron, sister, and mother. She images for them the transformed life they seek to live.

Over the centuries, a variety of branches of the Carmelites community have arisen—some apostolic and some enclosed—and many stemming from the desire for reform. Most notable among these are the Discalced Carmelites (the term means "barefoot") which came into being in the sixteenth century. Several of the most luminous teachers of Catholic prayer come from this tradition of Carmel: Saints Teresa of Ávila, John of the Cross, and Thérèse of Lisieux. There are other Discalced Carmelites as well who, while perhaps less well-known, have recorded their deep insights about the human longing for and relationship with God: Brother Lawrence of the Resurrection, Elizabeth of the Trinity, and Edith Stein are examples.

Teresa is perhaps best known for her writing on contemplative prayer, but she was a formidable reformer in her day. As a young woman, Teresa joined a large traditional Carmelite community of nuns in her Spanish hometown of Ávila. It was not that the life she found there was reprehensible, but as she aged, she struggled with the impersonal and institutional quality of the life and her own routine observance. Some of her discontent seems to have manifested itself in physical illness. But in 1554, she was touched deeply in prayer by a realization of Christ's sufferings and his wounded humanity and was drawn into a deep mystical relationship with her Lord. She began to dream of a more intimate, intentional community conducive to prayer and the soul-union that she was experiencing. She wanted it to be free of the rigid social conventions and extended family influences that so dominated usual convents; she wanted a life that would mirror the warmth, friendship, and intimacy of the life of the Holy Family at Nazareth. Teresa set out to create new smaller groupings of women where enclosure and simplicity would guarantee independence and facilitate deep prayer. Her heroic reforming efforts and unceasing advocacy for such eventually issued in the foundation of a new branch of Carmel. Her younger counterpart in the reform of the men's branch, John of the Cross, was actually imprisoned for his attempts to do likewise.

As important as they were as reformers, the more popular legacy of these two Carmelites is, however, their spiritual writings. John was a brilliant poet: his *Spiritual Canticle* is a masterpiece of the Spanish language. Along with his other books, *Ascent of Mount Carmel* and *Dark Night of the Soul*, John explores the depths of divine love as it transfigures a human lover. Teresa too was a genius at putting words, homey yet nonetheless profound, to the experience of the inner journey. Her *Interior Castle* describes with telling metaphors the way in which a spiritual seeker, striving to respond to the divine invitation, might gradually be embraced and united with God. Teresan Carmelite convents across America today are still characterized by their contemplative identity. The Web site of the San Diego, California, monastery says it well: "For us as Carmelites, there is only one 'doing': always to return to our inmost center, seeking him whom we love. It is in this doing that every other doing finds its value and meaning" (www.carmelsandiego.com).

APOSTOLIC TRADITIONS

As suggested, Jesuit theologian Karl Rahner has described the saints as pioneers of new forms of holiness in the Church in each historical era. This implies that the Spirit working in the Church is always generating something new, as well as assuring continuity with the treasure handed down from the past. This newness is not abandonment of what has gone before so much as it is the unfolding of the inexhaustible and ever-creative potential embedded in the tradition. New historical circumstances call for new responses.

Certainly, it is a very Catholic observation to observe that the faith and its various expressions in theology, ethics, lifestyles, and commitments respond to the changes in the world. For example, the present ecological crisis is not one that medieval or patristic or early modern Catholics could have envisioned. Nor could they have conceived of the moral and spiritual issues engendered by contemporary advances in technology. So the Spirit prompts a response in each age and place. The sixteenth, seventeenth, and nineteenth centuries are illustrative of this process as innovative apostolically oriented communities emerged.

In the early modern world, with the tragedy of the Reformation dividing Christendom, new types of religious life emerged, each with its distinctive charism, each prompted by the social and ecclesial needs of the day. Some of these experiments in new forms of Christian life preceded the actual Protestant-Catholic split. In fact, historians of the period note that reform in all areas of church life had been contested and discussed for several long decades before Martin Luther's 1517 critique of the misuse of indulgences simply served as the straw that broke the camel's back. Evidence of these reforming efforts was seen in the creation of new communities, among them the Jesuits, Ursulines, Capuchins, Theatines, Barnibites, Congregation of the Oratory, and Pirarists, variously founded to reform the clergy and to evangelize the laity by teaching, preaching, and performing good works. These innovative groups experimented with different life-style models appropriate to the active apostolate. They responded to the emerging needs of an increasingly urban society and eventually became the agents of the vigorous Catholic reform agenda. To counter the Protestant challenge and revivify Catholic society, they served as missionaries, teachers, preachers, catechists, and confessors.

Among the newly minted orders was the Society of Jesus, whose founder, Ignatius of Loyola, and whose distinctive spiritual practices we have already mentioned. The Jesuits wanted to be absolutely available for any sort of apostolic need as it arose in the vigorous reforming Church of the sixteenth century. Hence, they broke out of the classic monastic model and even eschewed the mendicant life. They dressed in the fashion of the time rather than in monastic dress, they were mobile, and through their absolute obedience to superiors, they were quickly mobilized in response to urgent apostolic needs. A company of well educated men, directly accountable to the pope, they took on the work of reforming early modern Catholic society. Especially, they became the great schoolmasters of the European elite, inculcating in their charges a commitment to the "more" and to doing everything for the greater glory of God.

Similarly, the spiritual development of the clergy was very much part of the larger effort of reform, and several congregations, notably Philip Neri's Oratory of Divine Love in Italy and the later French Oratory founded by Pierre de Bérulle, were founded specifically for the spiritual formation of diocesan priests. In addition, groups dedicated to the theological education of priests and the staffing of seminaries, such as the Sulpicians and the Eudists, were established in France in the later seventeenth century. These groups were responding to the critical needs of their eras. They were apostolic in thrust; in other words, they saw themselves as existing to perform a certain work, an apostolate. In similar manner, a number of women's orders with a teaching apostolate emerged. The history of the emergence of such communities is very complex, but they were the wave of the future. The Ursulines, founded in Italy in the early sixteenth century by Angela Merici, are a case in point. The education of young girls was foremost in this saint's mind, and she first envisioned herself and her small band of followers as consecrated virgins living in the world and serving God as teachers. Although the time was not yet ripe for such an uncloistered community of women to grow, the Ursulines nevertheless continued within cloistered walls and were the forerunners of many later teaching congregations of women dedicated to a particular work of apostolic service.

The Congregation of the Mission and the Daughters of Charity are representative of the reforming spirit as it ranged through early modern French society. These two groups, brought into being respectively by Vincent de Paul and Louise de Marillac, are part of what has become known as the Vincentian school of spirituality. They take their cue from the fourth chapter of the Gospel of Luke (16–24), which depicts Jesus at the beginning of his public ministry, standing up in the Temple in Nazareth and proclaiming the "year of the Lord" while using the words of Isaiah: "Good tidings to the poor, liberty to captives, sight to the blind, and freedom to the oppressed." This vision of a transformed world became the guiding vision of the Vincentians. To this end they preached internal missions (missions in Europe not on foreign soil), and engaged in ministry to the poor, orphans, and galley slaves. To effect the redistribution of societal resources, they enlisted the well-to-do in their efforts on behalf of the marginalized and dispossessed.

The spirituality of each of these active congregations was unique, yet they each saw themselves as imitating Christ, and thus bringing Christ to the world. While they refracted that impulse differently, the sense of participating in the redemptive movement inaugurated in the Holy Land was the same. An excerpt from the Common Rule or Constitutions written by Vincent de Paul and addressed to members of his Congregation of the Missions may serve as an example of this active spirituality:

> We read in sacred Scripture that our Lord, Jesus Christ, sent on earth for the salvation of the human race, did not begin by teaching; he began by doing. And what he did was to integrate fully into his life every type of virtue. He then went on to teach, by preaching the good news of salvation to poor people, and by passing on to his apostles and disciples what they needed to know to become guides for others. Now the little Congregation of the Mission wants, with God's grace, to imitate Christ, the Lord, insofar as that is possible in view of its limitations. It seeks to imitate his virtues as what he did for the salvation of others....

There are both clerical and lay members in the Congregation. The work of the former is to travel around through towns and villages, as Christ himself and his disciples did, breaking the bread of the divine word for the neglected, by preaching and catechizing. They also should urge people to make general confessions of their entire lives and hear these confessions. Their ministry also includes settling quarrels and disputes, establishing the Confraternity of Charity, staffing seminaries which have been set up in our houses for diocesan clergy, giving retreats, and organizing meetings of priests in our houses....The lay members help in these ministries like Martha in whatever way the superior wants them to. This help includes "prayers and tears," mortification, and good example.

If the congregation, with the help of God's grace, is to achieve what it sees as its purpose, a genuine effort to put on the spirit of Christ will be needed. How to do this is learned mainly from what is taught in the Gospels: Christ's poverty, his chastity and obedience; his love for the sick; his decorum; the sort of lifestyle and behavior he inspired in his disciples; his way of getting along with the people; his daily spiritual exercises; preaching missions; and other ministries he undertook on behalf of the people.

VINCENT DE PAUL AND LOUISE DE MARILLAC:
RULES, CONFERENCES AND WRITINGS

Like the seventeenth century, the nineteenth can be characterized as one of intense apostolic activity, as well as spiritual renewal. Innumerable groups, each with its own distinctive charism and history, yet each dedicated to building up the Body of Christ through service, were established. The apostolic spirit of this era was innovative, practical, and driven by compassion for Catholics in need. An example of one of the many communities focused on teaching are the Religious of the Sacred Heart. Their foundress, Saint Madeleine Sophie Barat, discovered her vocation amidst the chaos that the French Church experienced in the period following the Revolution. The Society she founded had the education of Catholic girls as its *raison d'etre*. Barat's collaborator, Philippine Duchesne, and several other sisters brought the order to the United States, where they established a network of schools noted still today for the intellectually rigorous, faith-based education they provide.

Similarly, the Sisters of Mercy, who in the present day describe themselves as "an international community of women religious vowed to serve people who suffer from poverty, sickness, and lack of education with a special concern for women and children," emerged in the apostolically-energized nineteenth century. This time the site was Ireland. Catherine McCauley, daughter of a prosperous Dublin family, was orphaned and became the companion of a wealthy childless couple, who left her their considerable fortune. Catherine's deepest desire was to serve the religious, educational, and social needs of women and children. Her congregation, formally established in 1831, answered the requests of bishops around the globe for women to serve in their dioceses. One result of the Mercy Sisters' apostolic energy was the creation of a network of hospitals and health care facilities across the United States.

Throughout Europe, religious congregations grew up to respond to the social and spiritual conditions occasioned by rapid industrialization. Two cognate communities, one of men and the other of women, the Oblates of Saint Francis de Sales and the Oblate Sisters of Saint Francis de Sales, were created to, respectively, educate young men and minister to young women who had migrated into the urban centers and were vulnerable to exploitation. Young people like these needed community centers in which to gather, job training, and opportunities for spiritual enrichment as well as basic catechesis. In this period, the spiritual writings of the late Bishop de Sales were once again gaining popularity. They spoke directly to the desire of the laity to grow spiritually, precisely in the midst of the work and family life, and they were widely promoted. Mother Mary de Sales Chappuis was superior of the Visitation monastery in Troyes. (The Visitation was originally founded by de Sales and lived his spirit.) The convent chaplain, Father Louis Brisson, and former student at the monastery boarding school, Saint Léonie Aviat, were the founders of these communities. In addition, with the collaboration of retired Bishop Louis Gaston de Ségur, an informal lay spiritual network was formed which radiated out from Paris across France. Historical sources indicate that mid-century, the Association of Saint Francis de Sales, whose aim was the spiritual nurture of Catholic laity through the study and practice of devotion in the spirit of the saintly author of the *Introduction to the Devout Life*, had over a million lay members. In addition, another Parisian priest, Father Henri Chaumont, helped devout lay woman, Caroline Carré de Malberg, establish a spiritual association for lay women who wished to nurture their Christian identities. Like their counterparts in the Association, these Daughters of Saint Francis de Sales took as their guide the Savoyard bishop's popular *Introduction*. But they formalized their program of formation and their organization for those who aspired to exceptional holiness of life, even while living "in the world." In the twenty-first century, the Daughters, also known as the Society of St. Francis de Sales, are present worldwide as a canonically recognized pious association.

While many of these and similar congregations of European origin helped serve the needs of the growing American Catholic population, there were native-born groups that sprang up on North American soil as well. Notable among these was the Sisters of Charity of Saint Joseph, whose foundress, Saint Elizabeth Ann Seton, was the first American-born individual to be canonized by the Church. Elizabeth, a widow with young children and a convert to Catholicism during the formative years of the American republic, had tried to support her young family by opening a school; it failed because of the anti-Catholic sentiment of the day. Soon she was recognized by the new country's first bishop, John Carroll, as a singular resource. With his help and the aid of the Sulpician priests stationed in the new republic, she opened the first free school for the poor in America and a boarding school for paying Catholic students in Emmitsburg, Maryland (established 1810). Her congregation was the first religious community of apostolic women founded in the United States and was inspired in its spirituality by the Vincentian charism, especially the Daughters of Charity. Seton is remembered not only as the foundress of her community, which in turn sponsored six other independent women's religious communities, but as the originator of the American parochial school system.

Issac Hecker was, like Elizabeth Ann Seton, a convert to the Catholic fold and, like her, drawn into apostolic engagement in the early American Catholic community. Hecker was convinced that the culture of his native land and Catholicism were not opposed, and he set out to evangelize both believers and non-believers with the aim of converting America to the Catholic faith. To do this, he founded the Society of Saint Paul the Apostle (1858), commonly known as the Paulist Fathers. Father Hecker sought to evangelize Americans using the popular means of his day, primarily preaching, the public lecture circuit, and the printing press. Their present publicity materials confirm the continuity of their mission.

> We give the Word of God a voice in pulpits and print, on radio and television, on the Web and the wide screen. [W]e seek to meet the contemporary culture on its own terms, to present the Gospel message in ways that are compelling but not diluted, so that the fullness of the Catholic faith may lead others to find Christ's deep peace and "unreachable quiet-

ness." Paulists do not condemn culture, nor do they try to conform the Gospel to it. Rather, we preach the Gospel in new ways and in new forms, so that the deep spiritual longings of the culture might find fulfillment in Jesus Christ. To this end, Paulists use printing presses, movie cameras, and web servers to give voice to the words of Christ—the Word Himself—to a new generation of Americans.

HTTP://WWW.PAULIST.ORG/

This mission of communicating the faith using the most current means available continues to be the charism of the Paulists.

The specificity of the American context provided the impetus for the creation of another Catholic congregation, the Sisters of the Blessed Sacrament. The daughter of a prosperous Philadelphia family, Katharine Drexel was moved by the destitution of persons of color she encountered on a trip through the West and Southwest. Seeing clearly that the conditions of these first Americans, as well as the poverty of African Americans, was the result of the deeply held prejudices of many of her countrymen, Katharine dedicated her life to the alleviation of racial injustice through the establishment of missions and schools. The current mission statement of the Sisters of the Blessed Sacrament reads:

We are confident in our God, we are enriched by the spiritualities and cultures of the Black and Native American peoples who have shared their life and love with us in mutual blessing. We are strengthened by our partnerships with others, and live in a spirit of hope, openness and discernment.

WWW.KATHARINEDREXEL.ORG/

The congregation she founded in 1891 continues her counter-cultural work of actively opposing all forms of prejudice, racism, and oppression through their various ministries.

Whether they come from Europe or are home grown, not all Catholic apostolic spiritual traditions are constituted as canonically recognized groups or as revivals of a specific spiritual charism (such as Salesian spirituality). During the nineteenth century, the diverse lay movement generally referred to as Catholic Action also emerged. Sponsored by the hierarchy and conceived as carrying out the Church's work in the world, Catholic Action groups mobilized Catholic lay persons across the globe and addressed a variety of social concerns. A number of lasting initiatives came out of Catholic Action, notably the Cursillo movement, which originated in Spain. Cursillos de Cristiandad (short course of Christianity) was founded in Majorca by a group of laymen in 1944 while they were refining a technique to train pilgrimage leaders. The purpose of the movement, which has grown greatly in the years since its founding, is to create small groups of Christians who will evangelize their environment with the Gospel spirit. A specific weekend experience aims to call forth a sense of being loved and called by God and helps to encourage a vibrant Christian identity. The Cursillo movement urges participants to commit themselves to spiritual growth, study, and faith-based action utilizing a variety of Catholic resources. Cursillo programs of spiritual and evangelical renewal have been widely popular in the United States and encouraged by the Vatican.

A more recently founded lay spiritual and apostolically oriented movement not associated with Catholic Action is the Community of Sant'Egidio. It began in Rome in 1968 at the initiative of a young man, Andrea Riccardi, who was then less than twenty years old. Riccardi gathered a group of high school students like himself to listen to and put the Gospel into practice, in imitation of the first Christian communities in the Acts of the Apostles and Saint Francis of Assisi. Since its beginnings, the Sant'Egidio community has grown to over forty thousand members living in sixty countries and has been designated by the Vatican as a "public lay association." The works undertaken by the community fall into several categories: prayer, spreading the Gospel, service to and friendship with the poor, working for peace, and bringing humanitarian aid to those who suffer in violent conflicts. Cultivating genuine Gospel-inspired friendship is at the heart of the Sant'Egidio enterprise. Frequent communal prayer; openness to the world while belonging to the family of disciples; advocating and caring for the materially poor, the forgotten elderly, and disadvantaged youth; working to eliminate war and violence which are the causes of so much poverty and suffering—these are the works upon which this Catholic lay movement focuses. In the United States, Sant'Egidio groups are presently found in Berkeley, Boston, the Twin Cities, South Bend, New York, and Washington, D.C.

One distinctively American Catholic lay movement mentioned previously, with its beginnings a bit earlier in the twentieth century, is the Catholic Worker Movement. Distinctly different, yet in continuity with the apostolic impulse, this loosely affiliated movement brought into being by American journalist Dorothy Day and French philosopher peasant Peter Maurin is mainly identified with its local Houses of Hospitality which, in various ways, offer shelter, food, sanctuary, spiritual nurture, and welcome to the urban homeless across the land. A personalist philosophy underlies all aspects of Catholic Worker life and teaches that all community members are worthy of respect and are to be to be thought of as brothers and sisters rather than as strangers. Nonviolence is another pillar of Worker philosophy and has often led community members to oppose wars and conflicts across the globe and to counter the structural violence of modern life through pursuit of the works of mercy. Besides Houses of Hospitality, the Worker movement has also sponsored communal farms and encouraged intellectual inquiry—what Maurin called "roundtable discussions for clarification of thought"—into social issues in its various locales.

This very partial catalogue of Spirit-led apostolic initiatives among lay and vowed Catholics is not merely of archival interest. What might be taken away from such a cataloging is a clearer picture of the way that the Spirit responds to the specific contours of time and place. The spiritual life is not simply about interiority, and about discerning God present in the human heart, but equally about discerning what God calls one to in response to the concrete realities of one's time and place in history. And always, Catholic spirituality is about the flourishing of the common good, as well as individual flourishing. In response to changing circumstances, varied traditions of apostolic spirituality emerged in the early modern and modern eras.

Different practices developed to support these new ventures. Perhaps the most sterling example of a tradition that developed practices for apostolic work is the Ignatian (Jesuit) tradition. In previous sections we have considered several foundational Ignatian practices: the daily examen or examination of conscience, the discernment of spirits, the retreat using the Spiritual Exercises, and imaginative meditation on Scripture. These were practices that could sustain a mobile ministry. At the heart of the Ignatian vision was a commitment to the mission of Christ in the world. One needed to be available to be sent where the need was discerned and have the skills to do the discernment. Especially important was the cultivation of interior freedom, a radical spirit of detachment to all that was not of Christ. Much more could be said of this, but the point here is that differing charisms—gifts of the Spirit—and differing traditions of spirituality have emerged over time and are integral to the Catholic story. *Unidivers* ("unity in diversity"), is the term that Saint Francis de Sales coined for this reality. As suggested previously, the term implies neither rigid uniformity nor individualistic anarchy. Rather, it suggests our deep identity in love in the Mystical Body of Christ and our capacity to respond to the dynamic life-giving energy of the Spirit.

MISSIONARY TRADITIONS

The early modern era was not only the era of reformation, it was also the period of western foreign exploration and colonization. Asia had been known to Europeans as trade had been carried on throughout the middle ages, but in this period, serious eastward religious evangelization began. The Jesuit Order especially sent missionaries to India, China, and Japan where their evangelical strategies mainly involved study and theological conversation with the elites of these cultures. But even more dramatic was the "discovery" of the New World to the west. Spanish explorers, along with Franciscan and Dominican friars and Jesuits, made inroads in the Caribbean and Central and South America, and eventually the southwestern region of what would later become the United States. French missionaries accompanied their countrymen in the exploration and colonial expansion in what is now Canada. These encounters, which were political and cultural as well as religious, were defining for both the colonialists and the native peoples of the Americas.

Catholic missionary work continued into the modern era; indeed, it continues today, although motivated by a somewhat different spirit. Examples of modern orders created especially to do foreign missionary work are the three missionary congregations: Society of the Divine Word, Sisters Servants of the Holy Spirit, and Sisters Servants of the Holy Spirit of Perpetual Adoration, all founded by German-born Saint Arnold Janssen (1837–1909). Feeling called to preach the Gospel in barely catechized regions beyond the borders of Europe, Janssen and his confreres launched missions in China, Togo (West Africa), Papua New Guinea, Japan, the Philippines, and Paraguay. Teams of missionaries were also sent out to care for the spiritual needs of poor immigrants in Argentina, Brazil, Chile, and Ecuador. The two Sisters' congregations were established to, respectively, work (especially in female education) and pray (eucharistic adoration within the cloister on behalf of the missions) alongside the Divine Word Missioners. Today there are more than six thousand Divine Word Missionaries who are active in sixty-three countries, more than thirty-eight hundred missionary Servants of the Holy Spirit, and more than four hundred Servants of the Holy Spirit of Perpetual Adoration.

The story of conquest is often an unhappy one, and the story of missions undertaken between the sixteenth and nineteenth centuries has many unhappy elements. Nevertheless, distinctive expressions of the Catholic faith were created out of the religious encounter of cultures. In the North American context, one is also aware of a distinctive Catholic community among Native Americans. At the Pine Ridge and Rosebud reservations in South Dakota, homes of the Oglala Sioux and the Lakota peoples, one can experience the way in which indigenous rites and symbolism—the acknowledgement of the four sacred directions, the use of herbal smudge sticks to purify an environment, the profound reverence for the sacredness of the earth—enhance and complement the Catholic ritual tradition.

One cannot go to India, the Caribbean, Latin America, or Africa today without discovering the rich diversity of global Catholicism born of the cultural encounters between European colonizers and those who were colonized. This same global diversity is very visible in the United States, also. Indeed, as a result of recent and not so recent immigration, most expressions of the world Church are present in contemporary America. Examples of some of these have been mentioned already in earlier sections. We are, of course, for the most part a nation of immigrants. The first Catholic Church within what is now U.S. territory was founded in Florida in the sixteenth century by Spanish explorers. Seventeenth century exploration by France brought Catholicism to the region of Louisiana, and the faith was propagated in the following century by the Spanish in the Southwest. Some of the most elegant reminders of this early Catholic colonial history are the string of mission churches that curve up the coast of California, the legacy of Franciscan missionary zeal.

Catholics were found on the colonial East Coast as well, as they were in the South and West: the Englishman Lord Baltimore set up his New World colony as a refuge for English Catholics in the mid-seventeenth century. After the establishment of the new nation at the end of the eighteenth century, Catholic immigration to the United States continued. Waves of immigrants from Eastern Europe and Ireland swept onto America's shores in the nineteenth century. A lot of these new arrivals were Catholics: Italian, Polish, Irish, German, Slovakian, and Czech members of the Church streamed in. That same era saw the annexation of southern (Texas) and western (California) lands that once belonged to Mexico where the church had already been firmly planted. In the twentieth and twenty-first centuries, Catholics have come into the United States through many portals, particularly from Central and South America, the Caribbean, the Philippines, and Vietnam, creating a colorful global mosaic of devotions, iconography, festivals, and spiritual practices.

This young nation, which was attracting so many immigrant faithful to its shores from across the Atlantic, was also the site of Catholic missionary activity from afar. After working as a schoolteacher and director of an orphanage, in 1880 Frances Xavier Cabrini and six other sisters took religious vows, founding the Missionary Sisters of the Sacred Heart of Jesus. Mother Cabrini was the first American (naturalized) citizen to be canonized by the Roman Catholic Church. Although her lifelong dream was to be a missionary in China, she was sent by Pope Leo XIII to New York City. There, she obtained the permission of Archbishop Michael Corrigan to found an orphanage, the first of sixty-seven institutions she founded in New York, Chicago, Seattle, New Orleans, Denver, Los Angeles, Philadelphia, and in countries throughout South America and Europe.

The missionary charism is a complex one: today foreign missionary work carried out by Catholics tends to focus on the practice of the works of mercy and justice. Gaining converts is not the focus of most contemporary missionary groups, as much as witnessing to the compassion and mercy of God through direct service to the suffering whom the world overlooks. Catholic missionaries serve all over the world. Even orders not established primarily for the foreign missions today engage in missionary work. For example, the Passionists (founded in 1740 by Italian Paul of the Cross and specializing in preaching internal missions) sponsor orphanages in Mexico, Honduras, and Haiti where they also operate a hospital to serve the desperately poor population in the capital of Port au Prince in the hemisphere's most impoverished nation. As for contemporary American groups founded specifically for foreign missions, the homegrown Maryknoll Mission Movement (the first branch, of priests, was founded in 1910 as the Catholic Foreign Missionary Society) sends vowed fathers, brothers, and sisters as well as lay missionaries to sites all over the globe. They engage in a variety of ministries; a few among their hundreds of initiatives are peace-building in war-torn areas, sustainable development such as rural women's cooperatives, civil and human rights advocacy, health care such as HIV/AIDS prevention and parish nutrition programs, and faith formation.

CONTEMPORARY AMERICAN SPIRITUAL TRADITIONS

There are other than chronological ways to chart the development of Catholic spirituality as we have been doing. It might also have been possible to point to certain geographical locations and cultural milieus that have their distinctive yet deeply Catholic spiritual approaches, practices, and themes. The Church is a global one, and from the beginning, the Gospel has been received in different cultural milieus and on different continents in varied ways. It is also possible to identify geographical locations that, in certain eras, have been especially spiritually alive. It is common to note that the sixteenth century is identified as the Golden Age of Spanish mysticism, which produced some of the greatest spiritual texts and figures of whom we have already made mention. Carmelites John of the Cross, Teresa of Ávila, and Ignatius of Loyola, founder of the Jesuit Order, hail from this golden era and place. Similarly, England, in the fourteenth century, gave us some of the most luminous spiritual writers: among them anchoress Julian of Norwich, whose stunning visions of the crucified and motherly Christ were recorded in her book *Showings*; hermit Richard Rolle, whose religious poetry sang of the love of God and humankind; and the anonymous author of *The Cloud of Unknowing*, who taught a compelling and transforming contemplative practice. The same century saw a florescence of similarly classic spiritual texts from the region around the Rhineland. German Dominicans Meister Eckhart, Henry Suso, John Tauler, and Margaretha Ebner, along with Flemish priest John Ruusbroec, preached, in various ways, a mystic plumbing of the divine ground, of being coupled with action on behalf of souls. In the same period and region, Cistercian nuns, like Gertrude the Great (known for her devotion to the Sacred Heart) at the monastery of Helfta and beguines such as Mechtild of Madgeburg and Hadewijch of Brabant who associated with them, produced remarkable poetry and prose works that sang of the encounter with divine Love. These women had spiritual forebears in the twelfth century monks of the Cistercian and Benedictine Orders throughout Europe who also produced classics of the spiritual life: Bernard of Clairvaux, William of Saint Thierry, and Aelred of Rievaulx wrote rhapsodically of the love song between the soul and God, and of spiritual friendship. Their contemporary, Abbess Hildegard of Bingen, recorded her astonishing cosmic visions and composed liturgical music that still compels today. Seventeenth-century France was similarly a site of spiritual florescence: Francis de Sales' beloved manual for laity, *Introduction to the Devout Life*, hails from this period, as do the towering figures of Vincent de Paul and Louise de Marillac, founders of the Congregation of the Mission and the Daughters of Charity, who made ministry to the poor their raison d'etre. Classic spiritual texts produced in eras of spiritual awakening like these are our inheritance, a treasury of personal and shared insight into the way the Spirit has worked and continues to animate the Body of Christ.

Students of the future will no doubt look back to the mid-twentieth century as the beginning of another one of these eras of intense spiritual awakening, in this instance, for the entire global Catholic community. The Second Vatican Council stands at the center of this awakening. While the vast effects of the Council cannot be adequately considered here, we can nonetheless give some attention to the ways that it both effected and intersected with uniquely American currents of spiritual awakening in our own nation. The United States, as suggested in the introductory section of this book, has a unique history in terms of spiritual movements of many types. From the perennial philosophy of the early New England Transcendentalists to the Protestant Evangelical Revivals known as the Great Awakenings; to the founding of new religious traditions like Seventh Day Adventists, Jehovah's Witnesses, the Church of Jesus Christ of the Latter Day Saints, and Christian Science; to the bewildering complexity of America's present day interfaith, ecumenical, and un-churched spiritual marketplace; the United States has been the site of spiritual ferment since its beginnings.

Amid this swirl, American Catholics have had their own influence. From within the Catholic tradition, profound currents of spiritual awakening were generated worldwide in the mid-twentieth century by the Second Vatican Council. The effects of this awakening are still with us on our continent today. For example, the council gave impetus to the Catholic Charismatic Renewal. The charismatic movement was not unique to Catholicism, but it flourished in a unique way. The first group of Pentecostal Catholics in the United States experienced the gifts of the Holy Spirit in the manner unique to Pentecostalism (notably by speaking in tongues) at Duquesne University in Pittsburgh in 1967 and at the University of Notre Dame in 1968. By 1972, Cardinal Suenens of Belgium personally encountered the charismatic renewal. It appealed to his keen desire to see the Church flourish, as in a new Pentecost, through the work of the Holy Spirit, a theme that drove the reforms issuing from the council. With the collaboration of Irish laywoman Veronica O'Brien, Suenens, who was a council moderator, sought and achieved papal recognition for the movement. While it has national leadership, on the local level, the Catholic Charismatic Renewal in the United States consists of thousands of men and women who meet for Spirit-filled prayer weekly, monthly, occasionally, or who form covenant communities. Members may be English, Spanish, Haitian-Creole, Korean, Portuguese, Vietnamese, Polish, Tagalog, or Italian-speaking.

The effects of Vatican II on the spiritual fabric of American life were and are, of course, much more widespread than the charismatic renewal. One aspect of the new Pentecost envisioned by the council was the renewal of religious life. Institutes and communities were encouraged to return to their sources to rediscover the particular charisms for which they were founded and to adapt their lives to better realize these charisms in a changing world. Religious were encouraged by Pope Paul VI's 1965 decree, *Perfectae Caritatis*, to "join contemplation, by which they fix their minds and hearts on Him, with apostolic love, by which they strive to be associated with the work of redemption and to spread the kingdom of God." One of the results of this widespread re-examination was that monasteries and religious communities took it upon themselves to make many of their spiritual resources, facilities, and practices available to the larger Church. Spiritual direction and retreats of all sorts became popular. Jesuits and other Ignatian-inspired communities offered Ignatius' Spiritual Exercises in accessible formats. The Cistercians promoted centering prayer; the Benedictines promoted *lectio divina* and liturgical renewal. Many institutes opened retreat houses and dedicated themselves to nurturing the prayer lives of those who visited. Other communities redoubled their apostolic efforts in teaching, preaching, and ministering to the poor and marginalized, all of which involved lay Catholics. Lay associate programs, Oblate groups, and Third Orders drew members.

Inclusion and encouragement of the laity was not brand new, however; the council had been anticipated early in the twentieth century by vigorous liturgical and biblical renewals, by the establishment of lay-run Catholic presses and magazines (notably Sheed & Ward and *Commonweal*), and by the formation of a spate of lay-focused groups like the Catholic Family Movement. These lay groups, known collectively as "Catholic Action," were intended to operate under episcopal direction with the assumption that the lay apostolate derived from that of the hierarchy. In something of a contrast, lay movements that emerged after Vatican II took their cue from the council documents that affirmed that the apostolate of all Catholics, in whatever vocation, derives from the sacrament of baptism, rather than filtering down from the hierarchy to the laity. This shift in emphasis encouraged greater lay responsibility and autonomy in action. The American bishops' pastoral letter, "Called and Gifted for the Third Millennium," further affirmed this view. This has had profound consequences for the spiritual development of American Catholics who have taken the bishops' charge to live the universal call to holiness with seriousness of intent. At the parish, diocesan, and national levels, lay Catholics hold leadership positions in spiritual enrichment programs, plan parish adult formation, are teachers and students in universities and colleges, direct spirituality programs, engage in spiritual direction and retreats as leaders and participants, and live vigorous, Spirit-filled lives.

The "universal call to holiness" enunciated by Vatican II was in part a result of the recognition of the essential role that the laity play in ecclesial life. The idea of a spirituality reflective of the centrality of work and family in the lives of most lay people was not entirely new. As we have seen, lay associations, Third Orders, and loosely-knit lay spiritual movements have been part of the Church's life for a millennium. But new attention was paid after the council, partly spurred by cultural changes and partly by shifts in the Church's own perspectives. The spiritual implications of marriage and of parenting have been recently explored in exciting ways, affirming that the family is the "domestic church," a small but authentic and foundational unit of the Body of Christ; the kenotic drama of the spiritual life is lived amid diapers, dishes, spousal intimacy, providing, sheltering, nurturing, and difficult in-laws. As theologian Richard Gaillardetz suggests:

> Any authentic spirituality, by revealing to us God's action in our lives, also discloses our truest identity; we "find" ourselves in our relationships with God and one another. A spirituality of marriage, then, will be concerned with the distinct manner in which God's transforming presence and action are encountered in our marriages. A marital spirituality should help us discover the ways in which, through our fidelity to the spiritual discipline of faithful marital living, we discover our truest identity before God.
>
> *A DARING PROMISE:*
> *A SPIRITUALITY OF CHRISTIAN MARRIAGE*

Similarly, theologian Julie Hanlon Rubio has explored the way in which the spirituality of the family is intertwined with classic ideals of friendship and the Catholic social teaching tradition by asking, beyond the love of spouses and children, ultimately what are families about? The answer she gives is a profoundly Catholic one:

> If husbands and wives have true friendship, their relationship should be about more than themselves. A marriage based solely on love and sacrifice of one to the other lacks the fullness of a marital friendship in which both spouses see their love for each other as the beginning of love for others. Spouses who are friends can attest to the richness of married love that goes beyond itself. Of course, in most cases marital love goes beyond spouses in the love for children.... Friends are called upon to care for a wider community, for the common good or the good of the polis. This understanding of friendship is also part of the Catholic tradition that asks families to look beyond themselves and thereby find their own commitments strengthened by love for others.
>
> A CHRISTIAN THEOLOGY OF MARRIAGE AND FAMILY

The Council did more than just rejuvenate the Catholic community; it also gradually contributed to the spiritual renewal of all Christianity. In opening the Church to the modern world, Vatican II emphasized that dialogue with persons of different religious persuasion was important. Especially was ecumenical dialogue with Christians of different denominational stripes encouraged. This would have profound consequences for spirituality. The Roman Catholic practices, texts, and resources for spiritual transformation, many of which had been accessible mainly to priests, women religious, and members of monastic communities until the mid-century, became seen as the common inheritance of all Christian groups. Methodists, Presbyterians, Lutherans, Mennonites, and other Protestants began to share in this inheritance. They were encouraged to mine their own traditions as well for spiritual practices and perspectives that had fallen into disuse. Simultaneously, as many Roman Catholics became aware of the often little known aspects of their own traditions, they were introduced to practices and texts from across the denominational divides. Today, the vast majority of American Christian spiritual resources, books, ad retreat programs, as well as spiritual direction, are conceived in an ecumenical light. Spirituality seems to be the place where doctrinal and ecclesial barriers, still separating Christians, are experienced in the generous light of common Christian seeking and love of God.

The interfaith arena has also been one opened up by the council. In a shrinking global community, formal dialogue between representatives of other faiths, as well as dialogue with Christians, has long been on the Catholic agenda. In terms of spirituality, this move to explore the interface between the world's great wisdom traditions such as Buddhism, Hinduism, Taoism, Native American traditions, Islam, and Judaism has gained momentum. That exploration had its seedbed in Catholic circles well before mid-century and Vatican II. Pioneers in interfaith spiritual encounter with Islam included Frenchman Charles de Foucauld and his admirer, scholar Louis Massignon. After several different careers and association with religious communities, Foucauld experienced his true vocation while living among the Islamic desert dwellers of Algeria and while establishing a rhythm of life that included hospitality to his neighbors, along with the contemplative practice of eucharistic adoration. He hoped to found a community dedicated to living alongside ordinary people, an expression of Jesus' own hidden life during his years in Nazareth, offering welcome to visitors whatever their religion, ethnic origin, or social status. Massignon, an influential Catholic scholar of Islam, helped realize the establishment of Foucauld's dream after the latter's death in 1916. The lay and religious fraternities that today take their inspiration from Foucault include Little Brothers of Jesus and Little Sisters of Jesus. Massignon's profound appreciation for the theological depth and spiritual wisdom of Islam helped pave the way for the Catholic interfaith openness evident in Vatican documents like *Nostra Aetate*.

Two other early Catholic promoters of interfaith encounter were Benedictines Bede Griffiths and John Main. The former was a British-born monk who spent much of his religious life in Christian ashrams in India, attempting to embody the wisdom found in both Catholicism and Hinduism. Griffiths affirmed what he saw as the contemplative core of all world faiths, while also affirming their essential differences. Main was another English Benedictine who was taught meditative practices using a mantra or sacred word to achieve stillness when he was assigned to Malaysia. He came to see this practice as closely related to contemplative practices taught by early Christian desert fathers. The spiritual organization, World Community for Christian Meditation, with its headquarters in Canada, is the outgrowth of Main's interfaith encounters.

Finally, among others, Cistercian monk Thomas Merton became engaged toward the end of his life in interfaith conversations with Buddhist practitioners. Merton's *Asian Journals* record some of his experiences in Thailand, his conversations with Tibet's Dalai Lama, and his correspondence with Zen master D.T. Suzuki. Today, this sort of interfaith encounter at the level of spiritual practice and experience between monks of differing religious persuasions continues in the form of the Monastic Interreligious Dialogue, sponsored by members of the Benedictine and Trappist Orders in association with the Pontifical Council for Interreligious Dialogue.

The spiritual renewal evident in the United States has also been affected by events in the southern hemisphere. In the wake of the Second Vatican Council, the Conference of Latin American Bishops met in Medellin, Columbia, and began a process of reflecting on the human and religious situation in Latin America and interpreting that situation in the light of the council. Sociological studies revealed that the economic and social reality for most Latin American Catholics was appalling. Theological reflection and pastoral action, the bishops decided, could not proceed without reference to that fact. If the Incarnation meant anything, it meant that the Divine and human were intimately connected, hence, the Church should make a "preferential option for the poor" in all that it undertook. The upshot of this shift in perspective has had profound consequences for spirituality. Liberation theology emerged with its emphasis on action for justice on behalf of and in solidarity with the poor and oppressed. An element of pastoral practice that comes from this movement is the formation of "base communities," generally consisting of the poor and a catechist who read the Scripture as liberating texts understood in light of their own experiences.

The Latin American experience has had consequences for Catholics to the north. A spirituality of solidarity and faith-based action undertaken on behalf of the poor has galvanized segments of the American Church. Many religious orders who minister in Latin America and overseas have created volunteer programs, especially for recent college and university graduates, that focus on direct service to those most in need. For example, the Claretians, a missionary order of priests and brothers founded by Saint Anthony Claret in Spain in 1849, see themselves today as dedicated to viewing the world through the eyes of the poor. They, like so many other congregations, sponsor a post-collegiate volunteer program stateside in which young Catholics work alongside the fathers and brothers. For Claretian volunteers, this means caring for the spiritual and material needs of recent United States immigrants, youth, and families. Those who volunteer with the Marianists (the Society of Mary), another congregation of priests and brothers founded by Blessed William Joseph Chaminade in 1817, live out their option for the poor and marginalized through a simple lifestyle and cross-cultural service in various U.S. sites like Hawaii and in Malawi, Africa.

271

One example of a Marianist service site is Loyola Academy, a Jesuit middle school for boys in grades six through eight that serves those who have the potential for college preparatory work, but who are in danger of failing to achieve that potential because of poverty, residence in distressed neighborhoods, or other social or economic factors.

This contemporary emphasis on the Catholic life as concerned with justice, service, and advocacy on behalf of the poor and voiceless has taken many forms. Inspired by the insights of the late Cardinal Archbishop of Chicago, Joseph Bernadine, who characterized the Catholic life ethic as a seamless garment that involved concern for life issues including war, poverty, abortion, racism, capital punishment, and euthanasia, a multitude of organizations that confront these issues have sprung up in the United States. These organizations are sustained by a Catholic sensibility about the common good and the sense that the Christ life is radically social. Additionally, "contextual" spiritualities, stemming from marginalized groups traditionally without a voice or from those whose voices have not been reflected in mainstream Catholic discourse, have emerged. For example, Mujerista and Womanist spiritualities that grow out of the experiences of Latina and Black Catholic women give expression to the hitherto unexpressed insights of significant numbers of Catholic faithful and bring to light aspects of traditional spirituality that may be oppressive to those on the margins of power. With other liberation theologians, including feminist and Asian liberationist writers, Mujerista and Womanist promoters such as Ada-María Isasi-Días,

Yolanda Tarango, Jeanette Rodriguez, Shawn Copeland, and Diana Hayes see the Gospel as liberating and preaching the reign of God, a reign of justice and peace where all God's children will thrive. Particularly, they question some of the essentialist claims of classic spirituality and theology which do not allow for the spiritual insights of different cultural and gendered experiences of encounter with the Divine. These newly articulated traditions within Catholicism are part of the creative, dynamic movement of the Spirit alive in the community.

More global justice concerns underlie other contemporary spiritual movements. Pax Christi USA, which functions with episcopal sponsorship and involves lay and religious Catholics alike, is the American wing of the International Catholic Peace Movement. It is dedicated to creating a world that reflects the peace of Christ by exploring, articulating, and witnessing to the call of Christian nonviolence, a practice that is both personal and communal and rejects war and all forms of violence and domination. A Jesuit spokesperson for Pax Christi USA, Father John Dear speaks with prophetic authority when he articulates the image that shapes his spiritual vision: "Jesus spent his life teaching and practicing creative non-violence...He commanded us to love our enemies and become blessed peacemakers. He forbade violence, killing and wars once and for all time" (*Put Down Your Sword*). He and others deeply engaged in the work of peacemaking see themselves, as have the spiritual masters over the centuries, as participating in the unfolding of the holiness of Christ in the world.

Similarly, and reflecting the turn in Catholic theology that would focus attention on the ecological crisis of the present, a growing number of Catholic nuns in the twenty-first century have increasingly "gone green." An eco-sensitive spirituality underlies the California ministries of the San Rafael Dominican Sisters who have a straw-bale hermitage at their Santa Sabina Retreat Center; the "Earth Home Ministries," an Oakland community garden project founded by two nuns from the congregations of Notre Dame de Namur and Immaculate Heart; and the Green Welcoming Center and Dining Hall, belonging to the Los Gatos Sisters of the Presentation. Social concerns about justice, human rights, peace, and ecological sustainability are strikingly prominent in the Catholic world today. They underlie many contemporary American spiritual traditions which have an apostolic orientation.

These examples do not exhaust the number of spiritually motivated initiatives that have flourished in the Church since the middle of the twentieth century. But as limited as they are, they give some sense of the rich and varied texture of the responses of the faithful who, within the context of the changing world, have lived into the deep desire at the core of their beings. As Father Rolheiser has reminded us, spirituality is ultimately what we do with the holy longing; which is simply to say that we are created to fulfill the Creator's own longing for the world, to mirror the Divine, and to love as we have been loved. The many traditions of Catholic spirituality and charisms that have abounded, from the first martyrs and desert ascetics to recent interfaith explorers and "green sisters," are all part of the vibrant spiritual dynamic alive in the Body of Christ.

The prayer that prefaces the U.S. Bishops' 1995 "Called and Gifted for the Third Millennium" is a fitting conclusion to this handbook on Catholic spirituality in all its historical and cultural diversity, but which is addressed in great part to American Catholics today. It reads:

> GOD
> of love and mercy, you call us to be your people,
> you gift us with your abundant grace.
> Make us a holy people,
> radiating the fullness of your love.
> Form us into a community, a people who care,
> expressing your compassion.
> Remind us day after day of our baptismal call to serve,
> with joy and courage.
> Teach us how to grow in wisdom and grace and joy
> in your presence.
> Through Jesus and in your Spirit, we make this prayer.

Sources Cited

Bonaventure: The Soul's Journey to God, The Tree of Life, The Life of Francis. Ed. Ewert Cousins. Classics of Western Spirituality Series. Mahwah, NJ: Paulist Press, 1978.

"Called and Gifted for the Third Millennium." The United States Conference of Catholic Bishops, www.usccb.org/laity/calleden.shtml.

Celtic Spirituality. Trans. Oliver Davies. Classics of Western Spirituality Series. Mahwah, NJ: Paulist Press, 1999.

Dear, John, SJ. *Put Down Your Sword.* Grand Rapids, MI: William Eerdmans, 2008.

Dogmatic Constitution on the Church (*Lumen Gentium*), Vatican Council II: The Basic Sixteen Documents, Copyright © 1996 by Reverend Austin Flannery, OP.

Gaillardetz, Richard. *A Daring Promise: a Spirituality of Christian Marriage.* NY: Crossroad, 2002.

Meister Eckhart, Teacher and Preacher. Ed. Bernard McGinn. Classics of Western Spirituality Series. Mahwah, NJ: Paulist Press, 1986.

Merton, Thomas. *Contemplation in a World of Action.* New York: Doubleday Image Books, 1973.

New American Bible with Revised New Testament and Revised Psalms © 1991, 1986, 1970 Confraternity of Christian Doctrine, Washington, D.C

Retrieving Charisms for the Twenty-first Century. Ed. Doris Donnelly. Collegeville. MN: Liturgical Press, 1999.

Vincent de Paul and Louise de Marillac: Rules, Conferences, and Writings. Eds. Frances Ryan and John C. Rybolt. Classics of Western Spirituality Series. Mahwah, NJ: Paulist Press, 1995.

Further Reading: Contemporary and Classic

Dear, John. *A Persistent Peace: One Man's Struggle for a Non-Violent World.* Chicago: Loyola Press, 2008.

Hayes, Diana. *Hagar's Daughters: Womanist Ways of Being in the World.* Madeleva Lectures in Spirituality. Mahwah, NJ: Paulist Press, 1995.

Isasi-Diaz, Ada Maria. *Mujerista Theology.* Maryknoll, NY: Orbis
Books, 1996.

Rodriguez, Jeanette. *Stories We Live: Cuentos Que Vivimos: His-
panic Women's Spirituality.* Madeleva Lectures in Spirituality.
Mahwah, NJ: Paulist Press, 1996.

Orbis Books in Maryknoll, NY (and Dartman, Longman,
Todd in London) have recently published a series of studies
on the variety of Christian spiritual traditions. The series
includes:

Chase, Steven. *Contemplation and Compassion: the Victorine
Tradition.*

Damian-Belisle, Peter. *The Language of Silence: the Changing Face
of Monastic Solitude.*

Lonsdale, David. *Eyes to See, Ears to Hear: Introduction to Ignatian
Spirituality.*

Martin, Thomas. *Our Restless Hearts: the Augustinian Tradition.*

McGreal, Wilfred. *At the Fountain of Elijah: the Carmelite Tradition.*

O'Loughlin, Thomas. *Journeys on the Edges: the Celtic Tradition.*

Short, William. *Poverty and Joy: the Franciscan Tradition.*

Woods, Richard. *Mysticism and Prophecy: the Dominican Tradition.*

Wright, Wendy. *Heart Speaks to Heart: the Salesian Tradition.*

Note: There are many translations of the classic texts in the Catholic spiritual tradition suggested below and throughout this handbook. Some noteworthy series of translations that can be recommended are the Paulist Press Classics of Western Spirituality series, which has many of the texts cited published under the author's name; the Institute of Carmelite Studies series on Carmelite authors; the Cistercian Publications translations of Cistercian Fathers; and the Modern Spiritual Masters series, published in the United States by Orbis Books.

Athanasius, *The Life of Anthony*
The Book of Margery Kempe
Elizabeth Ann Seton: Selected Writings
Issac Hecker: Selected Writings
Julian of Norwich, *Showings*
Martyrdom of Ignatius of Antioch
Martyrdoms of Perpetua and Felicity
Martyrdom of Polycarp
Rule of Saint Benedict
Sayings of the Fathers